4th AUGUST '05

To

WISH

BLESSING.

MY LOVE & PRAYERS

DENNIS

Gift *The* *of* *Faith*

Gift *The* of Faith

Short Reflections
by Thoughtful Anglicans

LaVonne Neff

MOREHOUSE PUBLISHING
A Continuum imprint
HARRISBURG • LONDON • NEW YORK

Morehouse Publishing
P.O. Box 1321
Harrisburg, PA 17105

*Morehouse Publishing is an imprint of the Continuum
International Publishing Group.*

All quotations from Scripture are from the New Revised Standard
Version Bible, copyright © 1989, Division of Christian Education of
the National Council of the Churches of Christ in the United States
of America. Used by permission. All rights reserved.

Other sources and permissions are listed in "Permissions" beginning on page 149.

Design by Wesley Hoke

Printed in the United States of America
1 3 5 7 9 10 8 6 4 2

Library of Congress Cataloging-in-Publication Data
The gift of faith : short reflections by thoughtful Anglicans /
[edited by] LaVonne Neff.
     p. cm.
Includes bibliographical references.
 ISBN 0-8192-1981-9 (pbk.)
 1. Faith. 2. Christian life—Anglican authors. I. Neff, LaVonne.
 BT771.3.G54 2004
 234'.23—dc21
2003013026

For my goddaughter Emilie Throop,
who was confirmed 21 June 1998
at age twelve

and

for my friend Lucille Leonard,
who was confirmed 31 May 2003
at age seventy-seven

❧

As you therefore have received Christ Jesus the Lord,
continue to live your lives in him, rooted and built up in
him and established in the faith, just as you were taught,
abounding in thanksgiving.

COLOSSIANS 2:6–7

Contents

Introduction

For by grace you have been saved through faith, and this is not your own doing; it is the gift of God.
—EPHESIANS 2:8

Faith is a gift from God. Because it is a gift, we cannot earn it, buy it, borrow it, or demand it. All we can do is wait for it, recognize it when it arrives, and put it to use.

The gift of faith comes in many sizes and in different forms. Some people receive a large gift all at once, while others get many tiny gifts doled out one day at a time. Your gift may not look a bit like mine, and we will probably use our gifts quite differently.

Differences are obvious in this collection of reflections, which span six centuries and several continents. The writers, all Anglican, represent many viewpoints:

royalist and Puritan, evangelical and Anglo-Catholic, rationalist and charismatic, conservative and liberationist. There are comments from people in various walks of life: bishops and professors, novelists and poets, people in business, musicians and queens. Bringing their differences together, they create a symphony of faith where both harmony and dissonance contribute to the total work.

I have left people's words alone, even if the spelling (from another country or another era) looks odd or the words sound sexist. Remember that until late in the twentieth century, *man* and *he* were assumed to include *woman* and *she*, and God was always spoken of as masculine. Few Anglicans today make those assumptions, but some still do. We are a diverse group.

Thanks to Father Matt Gunter, rector of St. Barnabas Episcopal Church, Glen Ellyn, Illinois, for opening up his theological library. Clearly a man of faith, he assumed I would return his rare books. I hope I did.

Chapter 1

What Is Faith?

"If you have faith the size of a mustard seed, you will say to this mountain, 'Move from here to there,' and it will move; and nothing will be impossible for you."

—MATTHEW 17:20

He said to Thomas, "Put your finger here and see my hands. Reach out your hand and put it in my side. Do not doubt but believe." Thomas answered him, "My Lord and my God!" Jesus said to him, "Have you believed because you have seen me? Blessed are those who have not seen and yet have come to believe."

—JOHN 20:27–29

We hold that a person is justified by faith apart from works prescribed by the law.

—ROMANS 3:28

Just as the body without the spirit is dead, so faith without works is also dead.

—JAMES 2:26

In an old fable, several blind men describe an elephant. One feels its tusk and says it is like a spear. One grasps its trunk and says it is like a snake. One touches its knee and says it is like a tree.

When people describe faith, they naturally focus on the parts of faith they have experienced, the aspects of faith that are most important in their lives. Some describe faith as *belief, knowledge,* or *understanding.* Others characterize it as *trust, obedience,* or *faithfulness.* Some emphasize the distinction between faith and works or between faith and the law. Others point out that true faith is always active and working. Many remind us that what is important is not faith itself, but the object of our faith—our faithful God revealed in Jesus Christ.

In this chapter, many different Anglicans express many different views of faith. Each of them is right, but none is complete by itself. Faith, like the legendary elephant, is broad and complex. To see the whole picture, we need to look at a wide variety of descriptions—keeping in mind that our vision is limited, and someone else's bizarre depiction may be just the corrective we need.

A Mighty Mustard Seed

Dennis Bennett (1917–91) *was a leader in the charismatic movement that started in the Episcopal Church in 1960 and quickly spread to other mainline Christian denominations. Charismatics emphasized the gifts of the Holy Spirit, including praying in unknown languages and healing through prayer and touch.*

We should not say that someone "doesn't have enough faith." Faith is not a quantity of something. It either exists, or it doesn't. You can't trust someone or something a little bit. You either trust him or you don't. If your trust or faith is hesitant, it isn't faith. This is why, in Luke 17:5, 6, when the disciples asked Him to "increase" their faith, Jesus pointed them to the mustard seed. He wasn't saying that they only needed a tiny morsel of faith; He was saying that a mustard seed, tiny though it was, could do mighty things if it had faith!

. . . But you can have faith at one moment and not the next, or you can have faith for one thing and not for another. To "grow in faith" means to become more consistent in believing, and to learn to believe in more ways.[1]

Climbing Out of Amnesia

Richard Nelson Bolles *is an Episcopal priest who, in 1970, self-published a manual for career-changers. Today, more than thirty years later, his book has sold over seven million copies and is the world's best-selling book on job-hunting.*

Religion or *faith* is not a question of whether or not we choose to *(as it is so commonly put)* "have a relationship with God." Looking at our life in a larger context than just our life here on Earth, it becomes apparent that some sort of relationship with God is a given for us, about which we have absolutely no choice. God and we **were** and **are** related, during the time of our soul's existence before our birth and in the time of our soul's continued existence after our death. The only choice we have is what to do about **The Time In Between**, i.e., what we want the nature of our relationship with God to be during our time here on Earth and how that will affect the *nature* of the relationship, then, after death.

One of the corollaries of all this is that by the very act of being born into a human body, it is inevitable that we undergo a kind of *amnesia*—an amnesia which typically embraces not only our nine months in the womb, our baby years, and almost one-third of each day (sleeping), but more importantly any memory of our origin or our destiny. We wander on Earth as an amnesia victim. To seek after Faith, therefore, is to seek to climb back out of that amnesia. Religion or faith is **the hard reclaiming of knowledge we once knew as a certainty.**[2]

Act As If You Trust

Robert Farrar Capon *is an Episcopal priest, theologian, and writer. Most of his books are about either God's grace or gourmet cooking.*

There are days when any honest Christian will admit that he thinks the promises of the Gospel are just so much incredible bologna. Even when he tries to catch the last handhold—the *fact* of the resurrection of Jesus—it gives way and he sees it only as the delusion of a handful of peasants, inflated to cosmic proportions by a tentmaker with excess intellectual energy.

But what he *thinks* has nothing to do with what he *does*.

No. Or yes. It doesn't matter. . . . There is no harm in thinking I am on the wrong bus when, in fact, I am on the right one—as long as I don't talk myself into getting off the bus. We have been offered a guide who says he can bring us home; either he can, or he can't. But what *I* think about him has nothing to do with *his* competence. I may believe in him with all my heart: if he is a fraud, it gets me nowhere. Or I may doubt him absolutely: if he really knows the way, I can still get home by following him.

You have failed to distinguish between *faith*, which is a decision to act as if you trusted somebody, and confidence, which is what you have if, at any given moment, you feel good about your decision. It is probably not possible to have confidence without faith; but it certainly is possible to act in faith when you haven't a shred of confidence left. Intellectual honesty is a legitimate hint for your own mental housekeeping; it has no effect whatsoever on things that already are what they are.[3]

Faith is an affirmation and an act
That bids eternal truth be fact.

—Samuel Taylor Coleridge
(1772–1834), poet

Belief in Christ as Savior

George Carey *grew up in a working-class family, failed an important school examination, dropped out of school at fifteen, and eventually became the head of the worldwide Anglican Communion. Converted at seventeen, he decided three years later he wanted to be ordained. Within fifteen months he made up all the schoolwork he had missed and began studies at Kings College, London. In 1991, after many years of serving as a parish priest and then as Bishop of Bath and Wells, Carey became the 103rd Archbishop of Canterbury—a job he once said he would not wish on his worst enemy! He retired in 2002.*

Faith has two levels: corporate faith *(fides)* and personal trust *(fiducia)*. Both are essential.

The faith of the church is necessary for Christian belief. I cannot go my own way; I am called to identify with the deposit of faith. For nearly two thousand years the Christian church has hammered out its belief structure, and we need to submit to it to call ourselves Christians. I cannot say, "I believe in Christ—a tremendous guy—but of course I don't believe he was the Son of God." That might make me a Christian camp-follower, but not a Christian. The Christian church is clear that we don't come on our own terms; we come on God's.

And the second dimension of faith is crucial too. It would be odd to say "I'm afraid I have no personal faith in Jesus Christ as God's Son. But if the church requires me to assent to it, I will do so. I'll let the church believe for me." . . . The Christian answer is simple. Your personal assent is required; no equivocation is allowable.

But what is the character of faith if it is personal and corporate? Essentially, it is belief in Christ as Savior. He alone has dealt decisively with the problem of sin, death and alienation.[4]

Six Impossible Things Before Breakfast

Lewis Carroll (1832–98), *whose real name was Charles Lutwidge Dodgson, taught mathematics at Christ Church, Oxford, and made friends with the three small daughters of Henry Liddell, dean of Christ Church. He immortalized one of those girls, Alice, in* Alice in Wonderland *and* Through the Looking Glass. *This story is often quoted by religious writers who want to explain what faith is* not.

"Let's consider our age to begin with [the Queen said]—how old are you?"

"I'm seven and a half, exactly."

"You needn't say 'exactly,'" the Queen remarked. "I can believe it without that. Now I'll give *you* something to believe. I'm just one hundred and one, five months and a day."

"I ca'n't believe *that!*" said Alice.

"Ca'n't you?" the Queen said in a pitying tone. "Try again: draw a long breath, and shut your eyes."

Alice laughed. "There's no use trying," she said: "one *can't* believe impossible things."

"I daresay you haven't had much practice," said the Queen. "When I was your age, I always did it for half-an-hour a day. Why, sometimes I've believed as many as six impossible things before breakfast."[5]

When I go to church, what doesn't
particularly interest me is the Creed,
although I find that I can say it.
The Creed strikes me as very much
like a political platform of some sort,
and I believe that's what it was.
What I respond to is,
"Lift up your hearts!"

—Richard Wilbur, poet

Wanting It to Be True

Barbara Cawthorne Crafton *is an Episcopal priest, a popular preacher, a retreat leader, and a writer whose articles have appeared in* The New York Times, Reader's Digest, Family Circle, Glamour, *and* Episcopal Life.

You just believe in all this stuff because you want it to be true! People who don't believe sometimes say that with an air of triumph, as if they'd just discovered the fatal flaw that will bring down the whole religious enterprise. As if the element of volition in faith were news.

But *of course* we want it to be true. That's why we're here. If we didn't want it to be true, we'd believe in something else. Faith is not compelled by facts or evidence. It is a matter of the spirit, not just the mind— although the mind is a useful thing, and it would certainly be hard to think about faith without it. We see the same things everyone else sees: the same wonders, the same miseries. We don't live in a reality different from other people's. We're all in the same boat.

Hardly anybody who was alive at the time Jesus was born believed him to be the Messiah. Just a few shepherds and three old men from out of town. Many people would see and hear him, but not believe—so many that, in a few years, it would be possible for his enemies to kill him without raising much of a ruckus at all. Modern people are not the only ones who have a hard time believing. And evidence doesn't seem to have much to do with it one way or the other.

Yet, some of us hear Christ and some of us don't. Something has happened that has made us want to order our lives according to his presence and not his absence. We see that the hand of God is the good that can come out of great evil, acknowledging all the while that this good does not make evil any less evil than it was before. We desire the presence of Jesus, and so we begin to see it everywhere. Christ is born in us, and so we are reborn into our own lives. The cross stands beside our own suffering, and so we claim the empty tomb as well.[6]

A True and Lively Faith

Thomas Cranmer (1489–1556) *was Archbishop of Canterbury during the reign of Henry VIII, when England broke with the Church of Rome over the issue of Henry's divorce from Catherine of Aragon. Cranmer supported a translation of the Bible into English, and he was a major contributor to the first Book of Common Prayer. After the deaths of Henry and his son, Henry and Catherine's daughter Mary took the throne. She forced Cranmer to sign a renunciation of his Protestant beliefs and then condemned him to the flames. On the day of his execution, he put his right hand in the fire, saying, "This hath offended!" This selection is from a book of homilies he put together for pastors to use.*

YE haue heard in the first part of this Sermon, that there be two kindes of fayth, a dead and an vnfruitfull fayth, and a fayth liuely that worketh by charity. The first to be vnprofitable, the second, necessary for the obtayning of our saluation: the which faith hath charity alwaies ioyned vnto it, and is fruitfull, and bringeth foorth all good workes. Now as concerning the same matter, you shall heare what followeth. The wise man sayth, He that beleeueth in GOD, will hearken vnto his commandements (Sirach 32.24). For if wee doe not shew our selues faythfull in our conuersation, the fayth which we pretend to haue, is but a fayned faith: because the true Christian faith is manifestly shewed by good liuing, and not by words onely, as S. Augustine saith, . . . Good liuing cannot be separated from true faith, which worketh by loue. . . .

All holy Scripture agreeably beareth witnesse, that a true liuely faith in Christ, doeth bring foorth good workes: and therefore euery man must examine and trye himselfe diligently, to know whether hee haue the same true liuely faith in his heart vnfeignedly, or not, which hee shall know by the fruits thereof. Many that professed the faith of Christ, were in this errour, that they thought they knew GOD, and beleeued in him, when in their life they declared the contrary: Which errour Saint Iohn in his first Epistle confuting, writeth in this wise, Hereby wee are certified that we know GOD, if we obserue his commandements. He that sayth, he knoweth GOD, and obserueth not his commandements, is a lyar, and the trueth is not in him (1 John 2.3–4). And againe hee sayth, Whosoeuer sinneth, doeth not see GOD, nor know him: let no man deceiue you, welbeloued children (1 John 3.6–7). And moreouer hee sayeth, Hereby we know that we be of the trueth, and so we shall perswade our hearts, before him (1 John 3.19–22).[7]

You can sing about the Light,
or you can sing about
what you see because of the Light.
I prefer the latter.

—T Bone Burnett, singer and songwriter

God Has Faith in Us

Alan Jones, *author of* Soul Making, *is an Episcopal priest and dean of Grace Cathedral in San Francisco.*

Is anyone or anything really to be trusted? I find it difficult to trust. I want to trust my fellow pilgrims, but I rarely do. . . . Trust is a gift, and the miracle of faith is this: God, our fellow pilgrim, trusts us. God believes in us. God has faith in us. It is God's faithfulness that enables us to have faith. Faith is the acceptance that we are trusted, that God believes in us. It is God's "amazing grace" that melts the ice around the heart and rescues us from our spiritual immobility. It is God's love that so moves in us that we are able to resist the forces of resentment in the world.[8]

Faith and Works Cannot Be Separated

William Law (1686–1761), *though ordained in the Church of England, lost his job at Cambridge and was not allowed to preach or teach because he refused to take an oath of allegiance to George I. He could still write, however, and his books influenced Dr. Samuel Johnson, William Wilberforce, and John Wesley, among many others. Law's best-known book is* A Serious Call to a Devout and Holy Life.

Salvation by faith and works, is a plain, and very intelligible scripture-truth. But salvation partly by faith and partly by works, is a false and groundless explication of the matter, proceeding either from art, or ignorance. What sounder gospel-truth, than to say, that we are saved by Jesus Christ, God and man? But, what falser account could be given of it, than to say, that if so, then we are saved, partly by Jesus, and partly by Christ; that Jesus does something, and Christ adds the rest. For is not Jesus Christ, as such, the one undivided savior, with one undivided operation? And who can more endeavor to lose the meaning, and pervert the sense of this gospel-truth, than he, who considers

21

Jesus, as separately, and Christ as separately, doing their parts one after the other, the one making up what was wanting in the other, towards the work of our salvation?

Now to separate faith from works, in this manner, the one partly doing this, and the other partly doing that, is in as full contrariety to scripture, to all truth, and the nature of the thing, as to separate Jesus from Christ. For as the one savior is manifested in and by Jesus Christ, one undivided person; so the one salvation is manifested, when faith is in works, and works are in faith, as Jesus is in Christ, and Christ is in Jesus.[9]

Trust in God's Unseen Power

Kenneth Leech *is a priest, writer, theologian, spiritual director, and activist. He lives and works among the poor in East London.*

The mystics . . . teach that the journey inwards is not simply a path of self-disclosure, but that it brings us to the discovery of God. For God is within, at the deepest centre of our being. . . .

The great spiritual tradition refers to the movement inwards as the Illuminative Way. It is a way of experiencing light through darkness, for the light of God strikes the human soul as darkness. But it is a creative, positive darkness, a darkness within which we can move. Darkness achieves what years of study cannot. It is essential therefore not to try to avoid or escape the darkness of spirit, for it is an important part of our growth towards spiritual maturity. . . .

The reason that the Illuminative Way is described in terms of darkness is simply that the clearer the light shines, the more it blinds and darkens the eye of the soul. It is a deepening of life in faith, and faith is essentially trust in the unseen power of God. This experience of trust is fundamental to life in Christ and to true prayer.[10]

Proof vs. Conviction

Mark McIntosh *is an Episcopal priest, a chaplain and theological consultant to the Episcopal House of Bishops, and an associate professor of systematic theology and spirituality at Loyola University Chicago.*

I know some theologians believe we can prove that Christianity is true. I think that trying to "prove" Christianity by making it look like a generic religion actually does more harm than good. In some ways, the truthfulness of Christian faith has to be left in the tender hands of the Holy Spirit, who alone can convince us and lead us into all truth. My hunch is that the Spirit is far more likely to convince by moving us to pray and help at the night shelter and take some kids who have never seen a cow out to the country than by brooding over rational arguments. While I am not willing to try to prove the truth of the Incarnation, I [believe] that it is coherent: that the mystery we are being led to adore has a kind of logic we can grasp. . . . Thinking about Jesus in terms of the Incarnation makes sense; the *truth* of it is something I think we can only know in the end if we are willing to let the Holy

25

Spirit work in us the mystery of Christ's dying and rising.[11]

Faith is that which rests on

him who is the truth—God.

Faith is from God to God.

It is not gained by man's own toil

or search or study,

but is given by God.

—Edward Bouverie Pusey (1800–1882),
priest, a leader of the Oxford Movement

The Distinction Between Faith and Rational Assent

John Newton (1725–1807) *wrote the words to America's best-loved hymn, "Amazing Grace." For many years the captain of a slave-trading ship, Newton only gradually came to realize the immorality of selling human beings. In his later years he became an Anglican minister and an antislavery crusader.*

You wish me to explain my distinction between faith and rational assent; and though I know no two things in the world more clearly distinct in themselves, or more expressly distinguished in Scripture, yet, I fear, I may not easily make it appear to you.

You allow faith, in your sense, to be the gift of God; but, in my sense, it is, likewise, wrought by the operation of God, . . . that same energy of the power of His strength, by which the dead body of Jesus was raised from the dead. Can these strong expressions intend no more than a rational assent, such as we give to a proposition in Euclid? . . . This is one difference, assent may be the act of our natural reason; faith is the effect of immediate almighty power.

Another difference is, faith is always efficacious, "it worketh by love"; whereas assent is often given where it has little or no influence upon the conduct. Thus, for instance, every one will assent to this truth, all men are mortal. Yet the greatest part of mankind, though they readily assent to the proposition, and it would be highly irrational to do otherwise, yet live as they might do if the reverse were true. But they who have Divine faith, feel, as well as say, they are pilgrims and sojourners upon earth.

Again, faith gives peace of conscience, access to God, and a sure evidence and subsistence of things not seen . . . ; whereas, a calm, dispassionate reasoner may be compelled to assent to the external arguments in favour of Christianity, and yet remain a total stranger to that communion with God, that spirit of adoption, that foretaste of glory, which is the privilege and portion of believers.

So, likewise, faith overcomes the world, which rational assent will not do. Witness the lives and tempers of thousands, who yet would be affronted if their assent to the Gospel should be questioned. To sum up all in a word, "He that believes shall be saved."

. . . Faith is the effect of a principle of new life implanted in the soul that was before dead in trespasses and sins; and it qualifies not only for obeying the

Saviour's precepts, but chiefly and primarily for receiving from, and rejoicing in, His fullness, admiring His love, His work, His person, His glory, His advocacy. It makes Christ precious, enthrones Him in the heart, presents Him as the most delightful object to our meditations; as our wisdom, righteousness, sanctification, and strength; our Root, Head, Life, Shepherd, and Husband.[12]

Trustful Reliance

J. I. Packer, *who was educated at Oxford and ordained in the Church of England, is a professor and preacher as well as one of the most influential evangelical Anglican writers today. A faculty member at Regent College since 1979, he is now semi-retired in Vancouver, B.C., Canada.*

The word "faith" . . . gets the idea of trustful commitment and reliance better than "belief" does. Whereas "belief" suggests bare opinion, "faith," whether in a car, a patent medicine, a protégé, a doctor, a marriage partner, or what have you, is a matter of treating the person or thing as trustworthy and committing yourself accordingly. The same is true of faith in God, and in a more far-reaching way.

It is the offer and demand of the object that determines in each case what a faith-commitment involves. Thus, I show faith in my car by relying on it to get me places, and in my doctor by submitting to his treatment. And I show faith in God by bowing to his claim to rule and manage me; by receiving Jesus Christ, his Son, as my own Lord and Savior; and by relying on his promise to bless me here and hereafter. . . .

Sometimes faith is equated with that awareness of "one above" (or "beyond," or "at the heart of things") which from time to time, through the impact of nature, conscience, great art, being in love, or whatever, touches the hearts of the hardest-boiled. (Whether they take it seriously is another question, but it comes to all—God sees to that.) But Christian faith only begins when we attend to God's self-disclosure in Christ and in Scripture, where we meet him as the Creator who "commands all men everywhere to repent" and to "believe in the name of his Son Jesus Christ . . . as he has commanded us" (Acts 17:30; 1 John 3:23; cf. John 6:28 ff.). Christian faith means hearing, noting, and doing what God says.[13]

Faith Is Whatever We Act On

Dorothy L. Sayers (1893–1957) *wrote a great deal of theology, translated* The Divine Comedy, *and was a friend of C. S. Lewis, T. S. Eliot, and Charles Williams. She is best known, however, for her creation of Lord Peter Wimsey, the aristocratic detective, and his eventual wife, writer Harriet Vane, who are featured in twelve novels and two books of short stories.*

In ordinary times we get along surprisingly well, on the whole, without ever discovering what our faith really is. . . . "When a strong man armed keepeth his palace, his goods are in peace. But when a stronger than he shall come upon him . . . he taketh from him all his armor wherein he trusted. . . ." So to us in wartime, cut off from mental distractions by restrictions and blackouts, and cowering in a cellar with a gas mask under threat of imminent death, comes in the stronger fear and sits down beside us.

"What," he demands, rather disagreeably, "do you make of all this? Is there indeed anything you value more than life . . . ? What do you believe? Is your faith a comfort to you under the present circumstances?"

At this point, before he has time to sidetrack the argument and entangle us in irrelevancies, we shall do well to reply boldly that a faith is not primarily a comfort, but a truth about ourselves. What we in fact believe is not necessarily the theory we most desire or admire. It is the thing that, consciously or unconsciously, we take for granted and act on. Thus, it is useless to say that we believe in the friendly treatment of minorities if, in practice, we habitually bully the office clerk; our actions clearly show that we believe in nothing of the sort. Only when we know what we truly believe can we decide whether it is comforting. If we are comforted by something we do not really believe, then we had better think again.[14]

Our Trustworthy Object of Faith

John Stott *has written so many books and articles that an entire book has been written just to list them. His best-seller is* Basic Christianity, *which has sold over three million copies in more than fifty languages. Assistant curate, rector, or rector emeritus of All Souls Church in London since 1945, Stott has traveled and preached all over the world on behalf of evangelical Christianity.*

There is much misunderstanding about faith. It is commonly supposed to be a leap in the dark, totally incompatible with reason. This is not so. True faith is never unreasonable, because its object is always trustworthy. When we human beings trust one another, the reasonableness of our trust depends on the relative trustworthiness of the people concerned. But the Bible bears witness to Jesus Christ as absolutely trustworthy. It tells us who he is and what he has done, and the evidence it supplies for his unique person and work is extremely compelling. As we expose ourselves to the biblical witness to this Christ, and as we feel its impact—profound yet simple, varied yet unanimous—God creates faith within us. We receive the testimony. We believe.[15]

Faith Makes Us Work

Jeremy Taylor (1613–67) *earned his B.A. at eighteen and his M.A. at twenty, the year he was ordained to the Anglican ministry. He soon became a well-known preacher, but when the English Civil War began, the Puritans imprisoned him three times. Taylor took refuge in North Wales, where he wrote* Holy Living *and* Holy Dying. *After the war ended, he became a bishop in Ireland.*

Faith makes the merchant diligent and venturous, and that makes him rich. Ferdinando of Arragon believed the story told him by Columbus, and therefore he furnished him with ships, and got the West Indies by his faith in the undertaker. But Henry the Seventh of England believed him not, and therefore trusted him not with shipping, and lost all the purchase of that faith. . . . No man could work a day's labour without faith; but because he believes he shall have his wages at the day's or week's end, he does his duty. But he only believes who does that thing which other men, in like cases, do when they do believe. He that believes money gotten with danger is better than poverty with safety, will venture for it in unknown lands or seas; and so will he that believes it better to get to heaven with labour, than to go to hell with pleasure.[16]

Personal Faith and Public Action

Steve Turner, *a member of All Souls Church in London, is a poet, a rock journalist, and the author of many books about contemporary musicians. In his most recent book he tells the story of the hymn "Amazing Grace"—written in 1772 by Anglican John Newton, turned into a hit single in 1971 by Episcopalian Judy Collins, and still today America's most popular hymn.*

Christ showed particular concern for the weak, poor, bereaved, alienated, exploited and marginalized, and it is right to expect to see that concern reflected in the art of his followers.

The effect of what U2 has said about personal faith in Christ would be considerably diminished if they hadn't been seen carrying out these commandments. I'm convinced that a lot of the respect that is now given to them has come because they are seen as men of their word. The gospel makes more sense to people when they can see it acted rather than only hear it spoken.

U2 has been in the forefront of rock music's involvement in global issues since 1985 when they appeared at Live Aid, a benefit concert for the people of Ethiopia. Besides Bono's personal visits to trouble spots and the band's collective involvement with organizations such as Amnesty International, Greenpeace and Jubilee 2000, U2 has released several powerful songs attempting to understand the plight of the world's bullied and broken.

"Silver and Gold" was a reflection on apartheid; "Red Hill Mining Town" entered the thoughts of a British mining community whose pits had been closed; "Mothers of the Disappeared" spoke on behalf of Argentineans who lost their children during the reign of the military junta. Of course, any of these songs could have been written by a nonbeliever. But even though compassion is not exclusive to Christianity, it is essential, and U2 has been right to make these concerns such an integral part of their work.[17]

Faith Brings Liberation

Desmond Tutu *wanted to be a doctor, but a medical education was impossible for a young black man growing up in South Africa under apartheid. So he became a teacher like his father, but then in the 1950s oppressive laws were passed barring blacks from attending state universities and denying black children training for anything except menial labor. Tutu did not want to be part of such a system, so he became a priest instead, and he worked for the abolition of apartheid by nonviolent means. In 1984 he was awarded the Nobel Peace Prize, and in 1986 he became Archbishop of Cape Town and head of the Anglican Church in Southern Africa.*

All life belongs to God. The Christian faith believes that God uses ordinary material things as vehicles for God's spiritual grace and divine life, as in the sacraments. Our religion is incarnational through and through.

William Temple, the great Archbishop of Canterbury, referring to this quality of the Christian faith said, "Christianity is the most materialistic of the great religions." We declare that we believe in the resurrection of the body and not in the immortality of the soul. The body, according to St Paul, is the temple of the Holy Spirit. Christians are not dualists who believe that matter is intrinsically evil, and therefore all God's created universe, material and spiritual, counts for us. The whole of life is important, political, economic and social, and none of these aspects is untouched by religion as we understand it.

It is part of God's mission and purpose for His world to bring about wholeness, justice, good health, righteousness, peace and harmony and reconciliation. These are what belong to the Kingdom of God, and we are His agents to work with Him as His partners to bring to pass all that God wants for His universe. He showed himself as a liberator God. When He found a rabble of slaves in bondage, then because He is that kind of God, He set them free as the God of the Exodus who takes the side of the poor, the weak, the oppressed, the widow, the orphan and the alien. . . . God can't help it. He always takes sides. He is not a neutral God. He takes the side of the weak and the oppressed. I am not saying so. I have shown it to be so in the Bible.[18]

Response More Important Than Knowledge

Evelyn Underhill (1875–1941) *became an Anglican in her forties. Known for her books on spirituality, especially* Mysticism, *she spent most afternoons visiting the poor or giving spiritual direction. When World War II broke out, she became a pacifist.*

No words in our human language are adequate or accurate when applied to spiritual realities; and it is the saints and not the sceptics who have most insisted on this. "No knowledge of God which we get in this life is true knowledge," says St. John of the Cross. It is always confused, imperfect, oblique. Were it otherwise, it would not be knowledge of God. But we are helped by the fact that all the responses of men to the incitement of this hidden God, however it may reach them, follow much the same road; even though they may call its various stages by very different names. All mean on one hand action, effort, renunciation of the narrow horizon, the personal ambition, the unreal objective; and on the other hand a deliberate and grateful response to the attraction of the unseen, deepening into a conscious communion which gradually becomes the ruling fact of life.[19]

I do believe that die I must,
And be returned from out my dust;
I do believe that when I rise,
Christ I shall see with these same eyes;
I do believe that I must come
With others to the dreadful doom;
I do believe the bad must go
From thence to everlasting woe;
I do believe the good, and I,
Shall live with him eternally;
I do believe I shall inherit
Heaven, by Christ's mercies, not my merit;
I do believe the one in three,
And three in perfect unity;
Last, that Jesus is a deed
Of gift from God. And here's my creed.

—Robert Herrick (1591–1674), parson and poet

Christ, the Substance of Faith

Robert E. Webber *is a teacher, writer, and speaker with a strong interest in worship. The son of a Baptist minister, he became an Episcopalian while teaching theology at Wheaton College. Since 2000 he has been the Myers Professor of Ministry at Northern Baptist Theological Seminary in Illinois.*

I often tell my students that the history of the Christian faith can be compared to an artichoke. The kernel is found in the very center, hidden by layers of leaves. The layers represent the traditions we have built around the truth, traditions that sometimes stand in the way of encountering the truth in its naked power.

Just as we need to peel off the leaves of an artichoke to get to its heart, so in the Christian faith we need to peel away the layers of tradition that take us to the heart of faith.

. . . I have come to appreciate all the traditions for what they are. They are not the truth, they are the interpretations, the layers of secondary truth which we have added to the common core of the faith that comes from the apostles and the primitive church.

The church that I now claim as my own . . . is a particular tradition, the Anglican tradition. But . . . Anglicanism itself is not the truth, it is one way of describing and living out the truth of Jesus Christ, living, dying, and rising again for the salvation of the world.

The actual substance of faith, the content that stands behind every Christian tradition, is Jesus Christ.[20]

Not under the Law, but in Christ

Charles Williams (1886–1945) *worked at Oxford University Press from his early twenties until his death at age fifty-eight. In addition, he wrote fantasy novels, poems, plays, literary criticism, biography, and theology. Along with C. S. Lewis and J. R. R. Tolkien, Williams was an influential member of the Inklings, an Oxford literary group. Williams's writing, blending psychology, philosophy, and mysticism, can be hard to understand, but he still has many ardent fans.*

The one practically certain thing about the early Church is that all the Churches, by whomever founded or taught, largely agreed. And they seem to have agreed with St. Paul about the explanation as much as he agreed with them about the fact.

The fact then had happened. The doctrine of grace was the statement of the fact; the fresh morality was the adjustment of the individual to the fact; faith was the activity that united the individual to the fact. And the fact was (among other things) that the law—the law of right living, of holiness, of love—which could not be obeyed by man had discovered a way of obeying itself in every man who chose. Man perished if he did not obey the law. Yet the law was impossible, and it could not be modified or it would become other than itself, and that could not be. What then? How was man to find existence possible? By the impossibility doing its own impossible work on man's behalf, by the forgiveness (that is, the redemption) of sins, by faith, by eternal life; past, present, future states, yet all one, and the name of that state "the love of God which is in Christ Jesus our Lord."—"The whole creation groaneth and travaileth in pain"; "God had concluded them all in unbelief that he might have mercy upon them all."

. . . "He hath made him to be sin for us, who knew no sin; that we might be made the righteousness of God in him"—"an exceeding and eternal weight of glory." In such words there was defined the new state of being, a state of redemption, of co-inherence, made actual by that divine substitution, "He in us and we in him."[21]

Chapter 2

The Leap of Faith

Faith is the assurance of things hoped for, the conviction of things not seen.

—HEBREWS 11:1

By faith Abraham obeyed when he was called to set out for a place that he was to receive as an inheritance; and he set out, not knowing where he was going.

—HEBREWS 11:8

Immediately the father of the child cried out, "I believe; help my unbelief!"

—MARK 9:24

Belief, trust, confidence, action—these are all elements of faith. But where does faith come from? Can we make ourselves believe that something is true, even without proof? Can we force ourselves to trust a God we have never seen?

Pascal, a seventeenth-century French mathematician, thought that belief in God was a safe bet. According to his famous *wager*, you risk nothing and stand to gain everything by believing in God, whereas you risk everything and stand to gain nothing by disbelief. Kierkegaard, a nineteenth-century Danish philosopher, went further: even though you can't prove God's existence, you must leap over your doubts and believe. The alternative to a *leap of faith*, he thought, is utter despair.

In fact, as the Anglicans in this chapter show, people come to faith in different ways. Some do indeed make a calculated bet, while others close their eyes and leap. Some feel surrounded by God's presence from their infancy. Still others remember a particular time when they simply knew, or trusted, or experienced God.

The Gate Will Open

David Adam *was a coal miner before becoming a writer and priest. Today he is vicar of the Holy Island of Lindisfarne, for fourteen centuries the home of monks and pilgrims. Every year thousands of people travel to this remote island off England's northeast coast to spend time in quietness and prayer.*

Every now and again "our eyes are opened" and we see beyond the narrowness of our day-to-day vision. This was expressed by Jacob when he awoke out of sleep, a sleep he felt he had been in all his life up to that point: "Jacob awoke out of sleep and said, 'Surely the LORD is in this place, and I knew it not.' And he was afraid, and said, 'How aweful is this place! This is none other than the house of God, and this is the gate of heaven'" (Genesis 28.16–17). Jacob had not been looking for this experience, it had suddenly opened before him. I believe that such experiences are offered to all of us at one time or another in our lives. But we in our turn have to be open enough to receive them.

Life is meant to be an adventure; change is a gift that we have to learn to use aright. In Celtic folk-tales a curse that could happen to a person was to enter a field and not to be able to get back out of it. To be stuck in that place forever. . . . The open gate is the opposite to this. It is the invitation to adventure and to grow, the call to be among the living and vital elements of the world. The open gate is the call to explore new areas of yourself and the world around you. It is a challenge to come and discover that the world and ourselves are filled with mystery and with the glory of God. It is the ever present call to become pilgrims for the love of God, to take part in a romance that will enrich our hearts and our lives. . . .

This gate will open to us in quite an unexpected way and show us a world we never dreamed was there, and yet it was with us all the time. It is not that a new world is born, rather that we have awakened out of sleep to behold the gate of glory.[22]

Using the Bridge

Mortimer J. Adler (1902–2001) *was a writer, philosopher, and educator who edited the* Encyclopedia Britannica *and the sixty-volume* Great Books of the Western World. *Born into a Reform Jewish family, he converted to Christianity and became an Episcopalian in 1984. A year and a half before his death, he became a Roman Catholic.*

Granted that the reasoning carried on in this book is an interesting philosophical exercise. Granted that it may result in some change of mind on the part of some pagans who thought they had no grounds for believing that God exists. Granted even that it makes the universe in which we live more intelligible by explaining its existence, which would otherwise be inexplicable and absurd, as contemporary existentialists would have it. What of it? What practical use or value does that have? How does that change the meaning of human life, or the course of our lives?

In my view, a philosopher cannot avoid such questions, or shrug them off. Nor should a philosopher be content to tell those who ask questions of this sort:

"Go and do as Pascal did. Turn your back on the God of the philosophers and take a leap of faith across the chasm; for, on the other side, you will find the God you are looking for, who will make a difference to the meaning of life for you and to the course of your own life."

The philosopher can do a little more than that. He can build a bridge to the other side of the chasm by attempting to show—by reason and reason alone— the affinity that exists between the God of the philosophers and the god of the faithful, as objects of thought. That he can do, but no more, and that still remains insufficient for religious belief and worship. . . .

Reason can build a bridge, but it cannot carry anyone across to the other side. Pascal's leap of faith across an unbridged chasm may not be necessary, but the encouragement and attraction of faith are needed to motivate using the bridge to make the crossing.[23]

A Heritage of Faith

Agatha Christie (1890–1976), *the creator of Miss Marple and Hercule Poirot, was the world's best-selling author at the time of her death, with sixty-eight novels, over a hundred short stories, and seventeen plays to her credit. Her play* The Mousetrap, *which has been running in London for nearly fifty years, is by far the longest-lived play in theater history.*

My mother delighted in new experiments.

Her own experiments were mostly in religion. She was, I think, of a naturally mystic turn of mind. She had the gift of prayer and contemplation, but her ardent faith and devotion found it difficult to select a suitable form of worship. My long-suffering father allowed himself to be taken to first one, now another place of worship.

Most of these religious flirtations took place before I was born. My mother had nearly been received into the Roman Catholic church, had then bounced off into being a Unitarian (which accounted for my brother never having been christened) and had from there become a budding Theosophist, but took a dislike to

54

Mrs. Besant when hearing her lecture. After a brief but vivid interest in Zoroastrianism, she returned, much to my father's relief, to the safe haven of the Church of England, but with a preference for "high" churches. There was a picture of St. Francis by her bed, and she read *The Imitation of Christ* night and morning. That same book lies always by my bed.

My father was a simple-hearted, orthodox Christian. He said his prayers every night and went to church every Sunday. His religion was matter-of-fact and without heart searchings—but if my mother liked hers with trimmings it was quite all right with him. He was, as I have said, an agreeable man. . . .

My own religious views were derived mainly from Nursie, who was a Bible Christian. She did not go to church but read her Bible at home. Keeping the Sabbath was very important, and being worldly was a sore offence in the eyes of the Almighty. I was myself insufferably smug in my conviction of being one of the "saved." I refused to play games on Sunday or sing or strum the piano, and I had terrible fears for the ultimate salvation of my father, who played croquet blithely on Sunday afternoons and made gay jokes about curates and even, once, about a bishop.[24]

The Only Starting Point

L. William Countryman *is an Episcopal priest, a professor of New Testament at the Church Divinity School of the Pacific in Berkeley, California, and the author of many books for Christians who would like to find a sensible and loving God.*

God says, "I love you right now, the person you are as well as the person you can become." We say, "That's all very well for you, but I have higher standards." Or God says, "I forgive you everything." And we say, "Go forgive somebody who needs it. I could give you a list." We resist forgiveness because we fear it will demean us. It will make too light of our hard work and our difficult virtues. Or it will treat our real faults too lightly. But God is not making light of *us*, God is making light of what bars us from living fully in God's love.

The message of forgiveness says to us, "Get over yourself!" Get over your goodness and your righteousness, if they threaten to keep you from full participation in your humanity. Get over your faults, your inadequacy, if they're what hold you back. Get over whatever it is that makes you self-obsessed, whatever makes you reject God's wooing of you, whatever makes you feel that you would rather not go in to the party, whatever makes you feel like you belong to some separate and superior race of beings, whatever makes you feel like an eternal victim, whatever keeps you from living a real human life, whatever makes you imagine that there's something in this world more important and more fundamental than love.

Instead, be loved. Why would you refuse it? Perhaps you do it out of pique because you think God isn't taking you seriously enough. Perhaps you do it out of shame and embarrassment because God is being kinder to you than you think you deserve. Either way, get over yourself. You are forgiven. Start there. In the whole universe, it is the only starting point there is, anyway. There is no reality deeper than God's overflowing love.[25]

A Huge Act of Faith

Esther de Waal *writes, lectures, and leads retreats focusing on Benedictine and Celtic spirituality. She lives in a cottage near the border of England and Wales.*

In the Prologue to the Rule St Benedict presents us with that vivid image of the Lord standing in the marketplace calling out to the passers-by: "Is there anyone here who yearns for life and desires to see good days?"

If I say, "Yes, I do", and if I set out with St Benedict as my guide, I have no illusions about what is involved. He tells me that at first the way will be hard and narrow. He does not promise me escape from pain, rather "we shall through patience share in the sufferings of Christ". But he also describes this way as "the way of life". He promises that as we run and make progress our hearts will become "overflowing with the inexpressible delights of love", until at last we reach our heavenly home.

To say Yes to this invitation and set out with St Benedict is an extraordinary affirmation. Yes is a daring word, one that requires courage. To say Yes implies risk. It means moving forward. . . .

It is not, and it never can be, a Yes said simply with the mind, an intellectual conviction. It has to be the Yes that comes from the heart, the Yes that I say with body, mind and spirit, the whole of my being. What this means is that I have to descend into the depths of myself, to the real self without the mask, the self that lets go of appearances, before I can say it. It comes from me alone, for it is my own unique and individual response to that invitation. That is why I often find it frightening. For it involves a huge act of faith, standing alone, admitting my total dependence. Yet at the same time I know it would never be possible unless I knew I was held up and supported by my brothers and sisters in Christ—the individual and the community held together in tension, something that we have all experienced.[26]

Faith Means Risk

Elisabeth Elliot *was a missionary in Ecuador when some Auca Indians killed her husband and several other missionaries. Elisabeth, believing that their work was unfinished, returned to Ecuador and befriended the Aucas. In this memoir she tells of the importance of faith in her decision to go back.*

There is no need for faith where there is no consciousness of an element of risk. Faith, to be worthy of the name, must embrace doubt. In our going into Auca territory there were risks aplenty, so far as we knew. There was also the ground of our faith, the Word of Him who is called the "Pioneer and Perfecter of our faith." Nothing less could have brought us to that place. I know that there are many who take similar risks for the sake of adventure or scientific study. I am not one of them. I am afraid the "moment of truth" would elude me altogether if I were to seek it in high adventure. I prefer to seek Him who said, "I am the Truth."

We knew ourselves to be completely in His hands. Not more so at that moment than at any moment in our lives. Neither were we any more doing our duty at that moment than at any other. But circumstances made us more conscious of realities.[27]

Missionaries must be ready at a moment
to put their lives in their hands
and go out to preach the gospel to others,
with no weapon but prayer,
and with no refuge but in God.

—George Augustus Selwyn (1809–78),
first Anglican bishop of New Zealand

Nudged Awake

Timothy Jones *was an adult when he was confirmed in the Episcopal Church. Today he is a priest in Tennessee. His many books include* The Art of Prayer, Celebration of Angels, *and* Finding a Spiritual Friend.

One day, years ago, something simple and quiet nudged me awake.

I was hitting my teens, coping with the normal energies and anxieties of adolescence. Momentous events unfolded around me—assassinations, campus sit-ins, a draft that threatened to send my brother to Vietnam. But like nearly everyone else in my Southern California suburb in 1968, I lived an ordinary life. I thought mostly about everyday matters—friends, parents, life at Columbus Junior High.

But late one October afternoon as I walked home from school, the God of all things made his presence vividly felt. It was simple, really. I had been noticing how clearly I could see the craggy hills in the distance after an autumn wind swept the valley clean of smog. A yellowing sun cast long shadows on the sidewalk. The breezy coolness felt good on my cheeks. And I sensed with sudden elation that God was *there*. As I say, this was no complicated encounter, the clouds did not form themselves into a sky-written message from the Great Beyond. I don't think I told anyone. But the childhood God I had lobbed prayers to, the being I had vaguely reverenced on Sundays, somehow became a compelling Presence. I knew deep in my soul, perhaps for the first time, that God *was*.

I couldn't foresee it then, but that encounter began to effect a change that would take years to fathom.[28]

My faith burns low, my hope burns low

Only my heart's desire cries out in me

By the deep thunder of its want and woe

Cries out to thee.

—Christina Rossetti (1830–94), poet

Conviction Comes with Confidence

J. B. Phillips (1906–82), *a vicar in the Church of England, prepared a lively translation of the New Testament in 1958 that is still in print today. His 1952 classic,* Your God Is Too Small, *challenged popular misconceptions about God and offered a reasoned alternative.*

Men and women by the thousand today are convinced that the One whom they serve is not a heroic figure of the past, but a living Personality with spiritual resources upon which they can draw. A man may find difficulty in writing a poem, but if he cries, "Oh, William Shakespeare, help me!" nothing whatever happens. A man may be terribly afraid, but if he cries, "Oh, Horatio Nelson, help me!" there is no sort of reply. But if he is at the end of his moral resources or cannot by effort of will muster up sufficient positive love and goodness and he cries, "Oh, Christ, help me!" something happens at once. The sense of spiritual reinforcement, of drawing spiritual vitality from a living source, is so marked that Christians cannot help being convinced that their Hero is far more than an outstanding figure of the past.

The fact that this conviction only comes to those who have centred their inner confidence on Jesus Christ seems to rob it of all validity in the eyes of the hostile critic. Yet if, by an effort of imagination such a critic would concede for a moment that the claims of Christ were true, he must admit that the phenomenon is logical. If Christ revealed the true way of living and offered human beings the possibility of being in harmony with the Life of God (i.e., "eternal life"), it must follow that anyone living in any other way is by that continued action incapable of appreciating the quality of real living unless and until he "takes the plunge" into it. A man may write and argue and even write poems about human love, but he does not *know* love until he is in it, and even then his knowledge of it only grows as he discards his self-love and accepts the pains and responsibilities as well as the joys of loving someone else.

"If any man will *know* whether my teaching is human or divine truth," said Christ, "let him *do* the will of God." Those who accept this penetrating challenge are convinced that Christ is alive.[29]

A Leap into the Light

John Polkinghorne *is a scientist, theologian, and author. In 2002 he won the Templeton Prize—an award similar to the Nobel Prize but "for progress toward research or discoveries about spiritual realities." Formerly a professor of mathematical physics, Polkinghorne is a priest in the Church of England and president of Queen's College, Cambridge.*

The ability of understanding to outrun explanation is intimately connected with the religious concept of faith. This is not a polite expression for unsubstantiated assertion, but it points to an ability to grasp things in totality, the occurrence of an insight which is satisfying to the point of being self-authenticating, without dependence on detailed analysis. Involved is a leap of the mind—not into the dark, but into the light. The attainment of understanding in this way does not remove the obligation to seek subsequent explanation, to the degree that it is available, but the insight brings with it a tacit assurance that such explanation should be there for the eventual finding. Such experiences are quite common among scientists. Paul Dirac tells us how one of his foundational ideas about quantum theory came to him 'in a flash' when he was out for a Sunday walk. He was too cautious to be sure immediately that it was right, and the fact that the libraries were closed prevented his checking it right away. Nevertheless, 'confidence gradually grew in the course of the night,' and Monday morning showed that his idea was indeed sound. The mathematician Henri Poincaré was more certain of his insight. An important idea came to him 'At the moment I put my foot on the step [of a bus] . . . I did not verify the idea . . . but I felt a perfect certainty.'

Not all illuminations of faith come in this peremptory Damascus-road manner; many will involve a growing conviction whose coming to maturity may not be datable. Their common essence is the attainment of understanding by the power of a whole, by intuitive grasp rather than detailed argument. . . . Involved in this movement of faith is the exercise of those tacit skills which Michael Polanyi rightly diagnosed as indispensable to the scientific enterprise and which give it kinship with all other forms of human rational inquiry. 'We know more than we can tell.' In this way it is possible to transcend the limitations of logical system-building.[30]

A Moment of Certainty

John Updike, *one of America's most celebrated living novelists, was born Lutheran but now attends St. John's Episcopal Church in Beverly Farms, Massachusetts. This selection from "Pigeon Feathers" is about David Kern, age fourteen, who is burying some pigeons he has shot.*

He had never seen a bird this close before. The feathers were more wonderful than dog's hair, for each filament was shaped within the shape of the feather, and the feathers in turn were trimmed to fit a pattern that flowed without error across the bird's body. He lost himself in the geometrical tides as the feathers now broadened and stiffened to make an edge for flight, now softened and constricted to cup warmth around the mute flesh. And across the surface of the infinitely adjusted yet somehow effortless mechanics of the feathers played idle designs of color, no two alike, designs executed, it seemed, in a controlled rapture, with a joy that hung level in the air above and behind him. Yet these birds bred in the millions and were exterminated as pests. Into the fragrant open earth he dropped one broadly banded in slate shades of blue, and on top of it another, mottled all over in rhythms of lilac and gray. The next was almost wholly white, but for a salmon glaze at its throat. As he fitted the last two, still pliant, on the top, and stood up, crusty coverings were lifted from him, and with a feminine, slipping sensation along his nerves that seemed to give the air hands, he was robed in this certainty: that the God who had lavished such craft upon these worthless birds would not destroy His whole Creation by refusing to let David live forever.[31]

O help me God! for Thou alone

Canst my distracted soul relieve;

Forsake it not, it is Thine own,

Though weak, yet longing to believe.

—Anne Brontë (1820–49), poet and novelist

A Call to Relationship

Frank R. VanDevelder, *formerly professor of biblical languages and theology at Virginia Theological Seminary, is priest associate at St. Stephen's Episcopal Church, Oak Ridge, Tennessee.*

The picture of the sojourner's life is the biblical picture of the life of faith—life lived on the basis of trust in the God who created us and who loves us. . . .

At the heart of the matter is a call, a word of personal address, calling one out of the world of idols and false securities and away from reliance upon anything other than the God who calls. This call is an invitation to a relationship, personal in nature, which contains both promise and demand. If the call is heard and answered, then the life that unfolds within that relationship will be full and blessed, a life of joy and anticipation, continually moving toward greater fulfillment of the promise. It is a life turned toward the future, ever new, ever unfolding in surprising directions. This is life lived "on the road." The life itself is a journey, and security is found not in attachment to particular places or things along the way, but in relationships—to the God who calls us, and to fellow sojourners.[32]

Life comes to us in increments,
and the process of letting go of what has
served its purpose opens the way
for us to enter into a realm of
even grander promise....
New levels of existence await us when
"the dark at the end of the tunnel"
opens into ever grander light.

—John R. Claypool, priest, writer, and retreat leader

My Heart Strangely Warmed

John Wesley (1703–91) *is known as the founder of Methodism, though he was an Anglican minister his entire life. (In his day Methodism was a method—a way to experience Christianity—not a separate denomination.) A very devout young man, Wesley struggled for years to do everything required of a Christian, but he always felt he did not measure up. While on a missionary journey to America, he met a group of German Christians known as Moravians, and he was impressed with their inner peace during a violent storm. A few years later, sitting in a Moravian meeting, Wesley himself suddenly received the gift of faith.*

In the evening I went very unwillingly to a society in Aldersgate Street, where one was reading Luther's preface to the Epistle to the Romans. About a quarter before nine, while he was describing the change which God works in the heart through faith in Christ, I felt my heart strangely warmed. I felt I did trust in Christ, Christ alone for salvation; and an assurance was given me that He had taken away my sins, even mine, and saved me from the law of sin and death.[33]

Come As You Are

Rowan Williams, *the 104th Archbishop of Canterbury, was born in Wales and was Bishop of Wales until 2002. The first Archbishop of Canterbury in over three hundred years from outside the Church of England, he is also the first Welshman to hold that position in over a millennium. Williams is a scholar who has taught at Cambridge and Oxford, speaks seven languages, and has written many books. He and his wife, theologian Jane Williams, are the parents of two young children.*

Coming to the Christ child isn't always simple. . . . People come by roundabout routes, with complex histories, sin and muddle and false perceptions and wrong starts. It's no good saying to them, 'You must become simple and wholehearted', as if this could be done just by wishing it. The real question is, 'Can you take all your complicated history with you on a journey towards the manger?' . . .

Don't deny the tangle and the talents, the varied web of what has made you who you are. Every step is part of the journey; on this journey, even the false starts are part of the journey, experience that moves you on towards truth. It won't do to think of Christianity as a faith that demands of you an embarrassed pretence of a simplicity that has no connection with reality; isn't this what so often leads people not to take Christianity seriously? As though you had to leave the full range of human experience outside the door (the stable door), while the innocent alone entered without challenge? . . .

Bring what has made you who you are and bring it, neither in pride nor in embarrassment, but in order to offer it as a gift. It's possible to say to God, 'Use what my experience and my mistakes and false starts have made me in order to let your transfiguring love show through'.[34]

*Most people are brought
to faith in Christ,
not by argument for it,
but by exposure to it.*

—Samuel M. Shoemaker (1893–1963), Episcopal priest and early supporter of Alcoholics Anonymous

Chapter 3

Living by Faith

The righteous live by their faith.
—HABAKKUK 2:4

[Paul and Barnabas] strengthened the souls of the disciples and encouraged them to continue in the faith, saying, "It is through many persecutions that we must enter the kingdom of God."
—ACTS 14:22

Since we are justified by faith, we have peace with God through our Lord Jesus Christ, through whom we have obtained access to this grace in which we stand; and we boast in our hope of sharing the glory of God. And not only that, but we also boast in our sufferings, knowing that suffering produces endurance, and endurance produces character, and character produces hope, and hope does not disappoint us, because God's love has been poured into our hearts through the Holy Spirit that has been given to us.
—ROMANS 5:1–5

We walk by faith, not by sight.
—2 CORINTHIANS 5:7

Faith may save a person from despair or damnation. It does not, however, make life easy. The prophet Habakkuk sees nothing but war and famine around him, yet he has faith. St. Paul's affirmations of faith in Christ are coupled with a realistic acknowledgment that the Christian life is a constant struggle. The "faith chapter," Hebrews 11, tells of faithful people who are persecuted and ostracized.

Anglicans tend to prefer gritty realism to sugary half-truths: "Too much honey doth turn to gall," wrote the great theologian Richard Hooker. The writers in this chapter are no strangers to the dark night of the soul. Human anguish is here in abundance: Doubt. Fear. Depression. Injustice. Pain. Anger. Conflict. Disillusionment. Death.

But the light of faith is not extinguished. "I believe because of the epiphanies," says a historian. "Only a God in whom I trust completely could get me through this grief," says a musician. "I draw strength from the message of hope in the Christian gospel," says a queen.

Living by faith is difficult, to be sure; but for these writers, living without faith is unthinkable.

The Path to Faith

Randall Balmer *is professor of American religion at Columbia University. He is also a prolific writer, a National Public Radio commentator, and the author and host of several PBS documentaries. The son of a fundamentalist minister, he joined the Episcopal Church as an adult.*

For me, the path to faith has been rocky and my steps uneven. I am plagued by doubts and fears and anxieties. I feel desolate, at times, and my cries to God meet with silence. I have been locked in a lovers' quarrel with my father, the preacher, for the better part of three decades, a quarrel over faith and belief and theology that has not so much abated as it has taken a different form since his passing. Like Abraham, I'm not always certain where I'm going on this pilgrimage, and my progress is slowed, I'm sure, whenever I pause to wrestle with God—or someone— lurking there in the darkness. My trajectory is rarely straight and not always upward. It resembles, at times, the woven, brown cord of a toaster trailing off the table. . . .

And yet, what sustains me is a sense, or at least the hope, of divine presence, that I am not alone on this pilgrimage, but I am in the company of friends who will pick me up from time to time, dust me off, and point me in the right direction. What sustains me is a suspicion that there is still enchantment in the world—in the air on top of a mountain, in the crunch of leaves beneath a harvest moon, in the dazzling colors on the flanks of a rainbow trout, in the sound of wind brushing past pine needles. What sustains me is the laughter of my sons. What sustains me is the delight of love and companionship and making love. What sustains me is the conviction that the journey brings its own rewards, regardless of the destination, that holiness is somehow imbedded in the process itself.

I believe because of the epiphanies, small and large, that have intersected my path—small, discrete moments of grace when I have sensed a kind of super-intending presence outside of myself. I believe because these moments—a kind word, an insight, an anthem on Easter morning, a chill in the spine—are too precious to discard, and I choose not to trivialize them by reducing them to rational explanation. I believe because, for me, the alternative to belief is far too daunting.[35]

The Soul's Safe Place

Nevada Barr, *who has been an actor and a National Park Service ranger, is the best-selling author of an award-winning series of mystery novels featuring Anna Pigeon, also a forest ranger.*

My sister and I, both prone to the occasional bout of depression, were discussing ways of handling it. Why, we wondered over the phone lines between Mississippi and California, couldn't we just relax, watch a little television and wait for it to pass the way we would with a headache? The difference was faith. Healthy people, when sick or injured, have faith that they will one day be well. It's faith that keeps their courage up, allows them to endure with patience and a degree of good cheer. Depression, by its very nature, robs one of faith. A major symptom of depression is the feeling it is forever.

I think this holds true for life in general. Those who have faith that life is good, that things will turn out for the best, that suffering is a necessary learning process, faith in *anything*, survive the torments of life better than those who have given up. Faith masquerades as courage, patience, kindness under stress, generosity, optimism—the things than can make or break a life. If this faith is misplaced—faith in one's own strength, in the abilities of others—there will come a time when it must be repudiated by human limitations. Faith betrayed is a bitterness so deep it scars.

Alcoholics Anonymous suggests merely that one have faith in a "Power greater than ourselves." By putting our faith outside the human arena we put ourselves in the way of God, a place where we must believe without seeing, trust without contracts, suffer without vengeance. In choosing faith in something over which we have no control, little knowledge, something we cannot taste, touch, or smell, we place that magical part of ourselves that is wholly good beyond the reach of everyday evils. Regardless of what happens to us, we have a place to go where we can rest in the surety that everything will turn out for the best, if not here then somewhere else: heaven, the next life, in joining the flow of the Tao. This faith, this safe place of the soul, allows us to meet life with courage, generosity, and optimism.[36]

Practicing Faith in New Ways

Diana Butler Bass *became an Episcopalian while a student at Westmont College. A seminary professor, writer, and retreat leader, she is also director of faith formation at Christ Church in Alexandria, Virginia.*

Over the last twenty years of churchgoing, I have learned a few things about faith, about hope, and, above all, about love. I still feel afraid occasionally. But I no longer fear the wrath of a vengeful and demanding God. Rather, I fear I cannot begin to comprehend the breadth of God's love. I fear I will not be able to give away enough love—to my family, friends, church, to the oppressed and disenfranchised—before my time is done. Life is too short for all its love, to really understand its transforming power. And I sometimes fear Christians will not rise to the challenge of our times, that we will fail to embody God's love in the world.

As I think about it, however, one lesson stands above all others: it is hard to be a mainline churchgoer. It is not, as some critics claim, the easy road to faith. It is hard being a pilgrim soul in a church learning to be a pilgrim community. Conflict, timidity, injustice, quiescence, institutional dysfunction, and fear of change have been the cup of mainline unfaithfulness. Because of our own shortcomings, we live in congregations where it can be difficult to feel God's presence. I am trying—we are trying—to hear, heed, and practice faith in new ways. But it can be tough to stay with it. For me, for all of us, it has been a strenuous journey.[37]

To choose what is difficult
all one's days
as if it were easy,
that is faith.

—W. H. Auden (1907–73), poet

God Is His Own Interpreter

William Cowper (1731–1800), *a celebrated poet, suffered from severe depression for most of his life. From 1765–1773 he lived in the town of Olney where John Newton (author of "Amazing Grace") was his pastor and his close friend. During these eight years Cowper wrote sixty-eight hymns. In 1773 his depression returned and he became convinced that God had cast him out. He never went back to church, and he spent the rest of his life trying to keep despair at bay by gardening, keeping pets, walking, reading, and writing. In this famous hymn, Cowper expresses his faith in God's goodness even when life looks dark.*

God moves in a mysterious way
His wonders to perform;
He plants His footsteps in the sea,
And rides upon the storm.

Deep in unfathomable mines
Of never-failing skill,
He treasures up His bright designs,
And works His sovereign will.

Ye fearful saints, fresh courage take,
The clouds ye so much dread
Are big with mercy, and shall break
In blessings on your head.

Judge not the Lord by feeble sense,
But trust Him for His grace;
Behind a frowning providence
He hides a smiling face.

His purposes will ripen fast,
Unfolding every hour;
The bud may have a bitter taste,
But sweet will be the flower.

Blind unbelief is sure to err,
And scan His work in vain:
God is His own interpreter,
And he will make it plain.[38]

A Faith That Guides

Elizabeth II *has been Queen of the United Kingdom for over fifty years. These words are from her Christmas message in 2002, the year her mother and sister died.*

It is often difficult to keep this sense of perspective through the ups and downs of everyday life—as this year has constantly reminded me.

I know just how much I rely on my own faith to guide me through the good times and the bad.

Each day is a new beginning. I know that the only way to live my life is to try to do what is right, to take the long view, to give of my best in all that the day brings, and to put my trust in God.

Like others of you who draw inspiration from your own faith, I draw strength from the message of hope in the Christian gospel.

Fortified by this and the support you have given me throughout the last 12 months, which has meant so much to me, I look forward to the New Year, to facing the challenges and opportunities that lie ahead, and to continuing to serve you to the very best of my ability each and every day.[39]

A Long Journey into Experience

Nora Gallagher *returned to church when she was in her late twenties, though a decade passed before she felt comfortable admitting this to most of her friends. A writer who has been published in the* New York Times Magazine, *the* Washington Post, Mother Jones, *and many other newspapers and magazines, she has written about her Episcopal parish in two memoirs,* Things Seen and Unseen *and* Practicing Resurrection.

To live in faith . . . [is] a long journey into experience and away from idealism. One imagines religion as making one "good," and various ideal ways of behaving are often touted in pulpits. But the opposite of sin is not virtue but faith. And none of it works without the weight of experience, knowing something as an experience rather than as an event that passes over the skin. How *this I* experiences *this event* and folds it into flesh. How a soul, as Margaret Drabble said, weathers into identity.

Faith is not about belief in something irrational or about a blind connection to something unreal. It's about a gathering, an accumulation of events and experiences of a different order. These experiences are gradually convincing enough, or you have paid them so much attention, they reach critical mass. The famous "leap" comes at the beginning, when there is not enough experience to justify the effort. Even then, something begins faith—a memory of a reality or of an experience that doesn't quite fit with everything else, the longing a soul has to find its shape in the world.[40]

Almighty Saviour,

had I Faith

There'd be no fight

with kindly Death.

—Sir John Betjeman (1906–84),
English poet laureate

Faithfully Asking the Question

Gail Godwin *has written eleven novels including best-sellers* A Mother and Two Daughters *and* Evensong, *ten libretti for musical works, and many short stories. Many of her characters are Episcopalians.*

"Where is God in all this?" I once typed angrily to him from seminary, after a week on the third-floor ward at St. Luke's Hospital when I was doing my Clinical Pastoral Education. "Twenty-five beds filled with rape, shooting, and dope victims, and here's this young woman of eighteen born to be beautiful, with oozing, fresh razor scars all over her face *and* sickle cell anemia, and the nurse in charge is withholding her morphine simply because she's a sadist exercising her power. . . ."

He wrote back, by return mail that time:
"Your question may be the only one that matters. Despite all the convoluted guesswork of theologians ever since Job's friends hunched beside him on the dung heap, 'Where is God in this?' (just the question itself alone, I mean) may be enough to keep us busy down here. Maybe the thing we're required to do is

simply keep asking the question, as Job did—asking it faithfully over and over, whatever ghastly thing is happening around us at the time—until God begins to reveal himself through the ways we are changed by the answering silence."[41]

I see heaven's glories shine,

And faith shines equal,

arming me from fear.

—Emily Brontë (1818–48),
author of *Wuthering Heights*

Faith Goes with Me Everywhere

George Herbert (1593–1633) *gave up a promising government career and became a country parson. Soon he was known as "Holy Mr. Herbert" for his preaching, prayer, and generosity, and the personal care he devoted to the members of his parish. He is known today for his mystical poetry, published after his death at age thirty-nine. These lines are from a poem called "Faith."*

. . . Faith makes me anything, or all
That I believe is in the sacred story:
And where sin placeth me in Adam's fall,
Faith sets me higher in his glory.

If I go lower in the book,
What can be lower than the common manger?
Faith puts me there with him, who sweetly took
Our flesh and frailty, death and danger. . . .

What though my body run to dust?
Faith cleaves unto it, counting ev'ry grain
With an exact and most particular trust,
Reserving all for flesh again.[42]

Not Always Joyful

Richard Hooker (1554–1600), *a theologian and clergyman in the Church of England, was as important to Anglican theology as Luther was to the Lutherans or Calvin to the Calvinists. In a time when some English Christians favored Roman Catholicism and others preached Puritanism, Hooker argued for the* via media: *the middle road between extremist opinions. Hooker's writing also influenced the development of English and American constitutional law.*

[People] often mistake one thing for another. St. Paul wishing well to the Church of Rome prayeth for them after this sort: "The God of hope fill you with all joy of believing." Hence an error groweth, when men in heaviness of spirit suppose they lack faith, because they find not the sugared joy and delight which indeed doth accompany faith, but so as a separable accident, as a thing that may be removed from it; yea there is a cause why it should be removed. The light would never be so acceptable, were it not for that usual intercourse of darkness. Too much honey doth turn to gall; and too much joy even spiritually would make us wantons.

Happier a great deal is that man's case, whose soul by inward desolation is humbled, than he whose heart is through abundance of spiritual delight lifted up and exalted above measure. Better it is sometimes to go down into the pit with him, who, beholding darkness, and bewailing the loss of inward joy and consolation, crieth from the bottom of the lowest hell, "My God, my God, why hast thou forsaken me?" than continually to walk arm in arm with angels, to sit as it were in Abraham's bosom, and to have no thought, no cogitation, but "I thank my God it is not with me as it is with other men." No, God will have them that shall walk in light to feel now and then what it is to sit in the shadow death. A grieved spirit therefore is no argument of a faithless mind.[43]

No Need to Wrap Faith in Cotton Wool

Susan Howatch, *a best-selling novelist, converted to Christianity in the mid-eighties and began writing the Starbridge series of novels about the Church of England. She lives in London.*

Christianity is about truth and making sense of reality. Christianity is quite grown up enough to take anything that you can throw at it. I'm not a fundamentalist in any way. I don't have to wrap my faith in cotton wool to keep it safe. It has to go out in the world and earn its living and be useful, helping people to a better life. I don't find it restrictive at all. In fact, I find Christianity a great force of illumination.[44]

Anger Affirms Faith

Madeleine L'Engle *and her dog used to walk to her office at the Episcopal Cathedral of St. John the Divine in New York City. There and at her home in Connecticut she wrote dozens of books for children and adults.* A Wrinkle in Time, *the first book of the Time Quartet, won the Newbery Medal in 1963. In many of her novels, young people find themselves in an alternate reality where they face good and evil, mysteries beyond explanation, and, above all, the power of love.*

God—God the Father—loved the world he had created so much that he sent his only son—that spoken Word who called forth something from nothing, galaxies from chaos—he sent him to dwell in human flesh, to accept all earthly limitations, to confine himself in mortal time; and when this beloved son begged in agony that he might be spared the cross, what did the Father do? No thunderbolts, no lightning flash. Silence was the answer to the prayer. NO was the answer. And Jesus of Nazareth died in agony on the cross; the love of God echoing back into the silence of God.

That is love? How can we understand it? Do we even want it?

I sometimes get very angry at God, and I do not feel guilty about it, because the anger is an affirmation of faith. You cannot get angry at someone who is not there. So the raging is for me a necessary step toward accepting that God's way of loving is more real than man's, that this irrational, seemingly unsuccessful love is what it's all about, is what created the galaxies, is what keeps the stars in their courses, is what gives all life value and meaning. . . .

[God] has a strange way of loving; it is not our way, but I find evidence in my own experience that it is better than our way, and that it leads to fuller life, and to extraordinary joy.[45]

Not About Safety

C. S. Lewis (1898–1963) *was riding on top of a double-decker bus when he suddenly realized he believed in God, and he was on his way to the zoo when he decided he was a Christian. A literature scholar at Oxford and later Cambridge, Lewis is best known for his religious books. His best-sellers include* Mere Christianity, The Great Divorce, Out of the Silent Planet, *and the seven-volume Narnia series featuring Aslan the Lion.*

"Is—is he a man?" asked Lucy.

"Aslan a man!" said Mr. Beaver sternly. "Certainly not. I tell you he is the King of the wood and the son of the great Emperor-Beyond-the-Sea. Don't you know who is the King of Beasts? Aslan is a lion—*the* Lion, the great Lion."

"Ooh!" said Susan, "I'd thought he was a man. Is he—quite safe? I shall feel rather nervous about meeting a lion."

"That you will, dearie, and no mistake," said Mrs. Beaver, "if there's anyone who can appear before Aslan without their knees knocking, they're either braver than most or else just silly."

"Then he isn't safe?" said Lucy.

"Safe?" said Mr. Beaver. "Don't you hear what Mrs. Beaver tells you? Who said anything about safe? 'Course he isn't safe. But he's good. He's the King, I tell you."[46]

Let us have entire faith
in the Divine arrangements
for the growth of spiritual life,
although they are to us,
in our present condition,
unfathomable mysteries.

—Thomas Gallaudet (1822–1902),
priest, founder of parish for deaf people

A Ceaseless Battle

Michael Ramsey (1904–88), *a professor of divinity who became Bishop of Durham and then Archbishop of York, was appointed the 100th Archbishop of Canterbury in 1961. Active in the ecumenical movement, he was the first Archbishop of Canterbury since before the Reformation to meet officially with the Pope.*

People sometimes ask me if I have ever felt like losing my faith. No: my faith is always part of me. But faith isn't a state of easy and calm security. It is an adventure of ceaseless battling with troubles: a peace of mind and a serenity indeed, but a costly peace and serenity in the midst of conflict.

After all, our world is a world of conflict, and faith is not an escape from it, but something which—in St. John's words—"overcomes it".[47]

A Long Discipleship

Robert A. K. Runcie (1921–2000), *whose family was not Anglican, was converted after following a girlfriend to confirmation classes. A World War II veteran, an Oxford-educated scholar, and a pig-keeper, Runcie became the 102nd Archbishop of Canterbury in 1980. The next year he presided at the marriage of Prince Charles to Lady Diana Spencer before 750 million television viewers.*

The Christian faith in a Living Lord is always part of a long discipleship. Thomas could not have said, "My Lord and my God!" after Easter if he had not said earlier, "Let us go with Him, that we may also die with Him." If you have walked with Him in Galilee, in the ordinary workaday world, and if you have in some sense died with Him on Calvary, and kept trust in the long, dark shadows of life, then you can accept the end of the Gospel story, too. If you have seen Jesus taking the sting out of death, then the completion and proclamation of that conquest over death at that first Easter are not incredible. Without these experiences, men and women will always laugh at Jesus and the Resurrection as did the sophisticated Athenian of old.

With these experiences Easter Day wins conviction but never loses its wonder and power to astonish us.[48]

Give me my scallop shell of quiet,
My staff of faith to walk upon,
My scrip of joy, immortal diet,
My bottle of salvation:
My gown of glory, hope's true gauge,
And thus I'll take my pilgrimage.

—Sir Walter Raleigh (c. 1552–1618),
explorer and poet

Daily Postponement

Luci Shaw, *an active parishioner at St. Paul's Episcopal Church, Bellingham, Washington, is, among other things, a mother, grandmother, poet, teacher, editor, publisher, retreat leader, and speaker.*

Faith

Spring is a promise
in the closed fist
of a long winter. All
we have got is a raw
slant of light at a low
angle, a rising river
of wind, and an icy rain
that drowns out green
in a tide of mud. It is
the daily postponement
that disillusions. (Once
again the performance
has been cancelled by
the management.) We live
on legends of old

springs. Each evening
brings only remote possibilities of
renewal: "Maybe
tomorrow." But the
evening and the morning
are the umpteenth day
and the god of sunlit
Eden still looks
on the weather
and calls it good.[49]

Our doubts are traitors,

And make us lose the good

we oft might win,

By fearing to attempt.

—William Shakespeare (1564–1616),
playwright and novelist

Filling Our Hearts with Faith

Alexandra Stoddard *is an interior designer, ardent gardener, and self-described "philosopher of contemporary living." She has written over twenty books on beauty, joy, and spirituality.*

Have we forgotten that meaningful living takes time? The simple, quiet graces of a well-lived life have been abandoned. The nonmaterial things you and I can't buy and sell are at the very core of our sense of freedom and joy. Shooting the waves at the beach after a storm, walking through the woods at sunrise, sitting quietly alone in a garden, having a siesta with your spouse, are not wastes of time. If we don't take time to wonder, to stargaze, to be in awe of nature's sheer majesty, we're focusing on all the problems mankind brings to us that are less important in the long run. We should feel free to spend more time in contemplation, prayer, and meditation, when we fill our own hearts with light and faith and hope. We don't have to go to a chapel or a synagogue or a mosque to do this. We can meditate standing over the dishes in the kitchen sink, or fall to our knees in appreciation of our blessings as we wipe up the bathroom floor after a bath.[50]

I Faintly Trust

Alfred Lord Tennyson (1809–92), *the son of an English clergyman, was appointed Britain's poet laureate in 1850. That same year he wrote* In Memoriam, *a long poem reflecting his best friend's death seventeen years before. In the poem, Tennyson reaches out to God in faith, in spite of a tragedy he cannot understand.*

Strong Son of God, immortal Love,
    Whom we, that have not seen thy face,
    By faith, and faith alone, embrace,
Believing where we cannot prove;

. . . .

Thou wilt not leave us in the dust:
    Thou madest man, he knows not why,
    He thinks he was not made to die;
And thou hast made him: thou art just.

. . . .

We have but faith: we cannot know,
    For knowledge is of things we see;
    And yet we trust it comes from thee,
A beam in darkness: let it grow.

. . . .

I stretch lame hands of faith, and grope,
    And gather dust and chaff, and call
    To what I feel is Lord of all,
And faintly trust the larger hope.[51]

No coward soul is mine,

No trembler in the world's

storm-troubled sphere;

A Christian is an oak

flourishing in winter.

—Thomas Traherne (c. 1636–74), poet and priest

Keeping the Faith

Phyllis Tickle, *formerly religion editor for* Publishers Weekly, *is one of America's most often quoted authorities on contemporary religious experience. Her many books include a three-volume set on fixed-hour prayer,* The Divine Hours. *Having first set foot in an Episcopal church at the age of seventeen, she now cheerfully tells audiences, "I'm so Episcopalian I'm dangerous!" This excerpt is from* A Stitch and a Prayer, *a story about the time her father made a coverlet.*

By the spring of my eleventh year when Normandy's beaches had been successfully stormed and fear was a less ready guest, my mother had taken to quipping that if the War did not end soon, the coverlet would exceed even the reaches of the bed. My father was . . . not to be dissuaded. His weaving and sewing no longer had anything to do either with craft or with the coverlet. They had, instead, become a discipline, and we all knew it.

Each stitch securing the petals of a rosette, each thread woven to fill in a center, each loop catching one into pattern . . . every individual flash of needle or hook, in fact . . . had been translated over the slow years into tangible prayer. So long as he stitched, my father kept the faith with those who could not—kept it until, as he so biblically said, "this indignation be over-past."

By V-J Day, when he tied off his last stitch, the rosettes had indeed grown to cover the bed literally from the floor on one side to the floor on the other side and from the floor at the bed's foot to the edge of its head, back again to cover the doubled pillows and then up, over, and back around them. He had kept the faith.[52]

Faith, mighty faith, the promise sees,
And looks to that alone;
Laughs at impossibilities,
And cries, It shall be done.

—Charles Wesley (1707–88),
Anglican deacon and hymn writer

Chapter 4

The Company of the Faithful

Just then some people were carrying a paralyzed man lying on a bed. When Jesus saw their faith, he said to the paralytic, "Take heart, son; your sins are forgiven."

—MATTHEW 9:2

I am longing to see you so that I may share with you some spiritual gift to strengthen you—or rather so that we may be mutually encouraged by each other's faith, both yours and mine.

—ROMANS 1:11–12

We must always give thanks to God for you, brothers and sisters, as is right, because your faith is growing abundantly, and the love of everyone of you for one another is increasing.

—2 THESSALONIANS 1:3

To Anglicans, church is very important. Week by week we come together as the body of Christ to celebrate the liturgy. Together we are nourished by the sacrament of Christ's body and blood. We gather to celebrate baptisms, confirmations, weddings, and ordinations. Together we grieve when loved ones die, and together we affirm our hope in the resurrection.

We pray in private, but we also practice *common* prayer. We pray for one another when someone needs healing of body or spirit. In the company of the faithful, we confess our sins and receive assurance of God's forgiveness. "Regard not our sins, but the faith of your church," we pray.

Together we hear the Word, and as a community we preserve, interpret, and pass on our ancient tradition. Relating to other imperfect saints, we are constantly challenged to grow in grace. Together we gain strength to take God's love into the world. Alone, we can do little, but when we gather in Christ's name, we become the body of our Lord, the sacrament of Christ—taken and blessed, broken and given for others.

Their Faith Has Made Me Whole

Robert Benson *became an Episcopalian as an adult, and now he writes books and leads retreats on spiritual themes. He is especially fond of baseball, bookstores, and Italian food. This excerpt is from an essay on his struggle with clinical depression.*

In the dark days when the Christ came to me as I lay there on my mat in the glare of the brake lights . . . begging alms at the city gate, or beside the pool whose waters promised healing if only I could reach them in time, or along the road where one could make mud for the eyes from spittle and dirt, or on the road to Mary and Martha's house, where the crowd jockeyed for position and a good seat, or in the tomb with Lazarus himself, wrapped in bandages, beginning to rot, alone in the dark—on the day when Christ said to me, "Do you want to be healed?" it was Norma who kept saying yes, not me. I was too tired, too ill, too afraid, too uncertain, too ready to die. It was Norma and my sister and my friends and a couple of dozen strangers who took me to the Healer.

"Your faith has made you whole," said Jesus to one

he had healed. In fact, in many cases it was the faith of those who came running through the town to tell the cripple that the Healer was nearby and convinced him that it was worth the effort to try and get there. It was the faith of those who carried the litter, pushed through the crowd, tore off the roof tiles, lifted the litter, struggled across the roof in the sun, lowered the rope, and ran downstairs to tell Jesus that the man who was coming through the roof was ready to be healed, whether the man knew it or not. It was their faith, or hope or desire or concern or wild dream or crazy idea, or something. In the end, it was their love for the cripple that made him whole.[53]

Faith and Obedience Forever

Phillips Brooks (1835–93) *was rector of Trinity Church, Boston, before becoming the Episcopal Bishop of Massachusetts. Today he is remembered as author of "O Little Town of Bethlehem," but in the nineteenth century he was best known for his advocacy of freeing the slaves. A popular preacher, he sold over 200,000 copies of his first book of sermons.*

O young disciples, whatever other kind of falseness to your faith you may fall into, may you be saved at least from ever being ashamed of it. It is the noblest, the divinest, thing on earth. You may have only got hold of the very borders of it, but if in any true sense you can say, "Jesus is the Lord," you have set foot into the region wherein man lives his completest life. Go on, without one thought or dream of turning back, and with no shamefaced hiding of the new mastery under which you are trying to live. If your Christian service is too small in its degree for you to boast of, it is too precious in its kind for you to be ashamed of. Go on forever craving and forever winning more faith and obedience, and so learning more and more forever that faith and obedience are the glory and crown of human life.[54]

At the Altar

Kate Young Caley *is a writer, teacher, and mother who came to the Episcopal Church after many years of searching.*

I walk well-known steps to receive the earthly elements of bread and wine, which change in a way I do not need to understand, into the very presence of Christ. . . .

I bring myself and everything I have ever been to the altar.

I cup my hands and lift them silently and humbly to receive the essence. The priest places the bread tenderly, the way I might have fed our lambs. I taste the plainness of wafer and the mystery of Communion as I work my tongue and teeth around the gift, never quite comprehending; and never minding that I don't. God comes to me anyway.

And then the shared cup. The priest approaches, tilting silver toward my lips and my mouth fills with wine, and my head warms, and my throat, and I look up to regard the tangled vines of bittersweet wound at the base of each altar candle, at the open tabernacle, and the cross. I take in all of the richness of color and warm wine, of candles flickering in the mixture of the altar's shadows and morning light, of voices lifted beyond us toward Him. It is only a moment, but it is enough.

I feel my knees stiffen on the lumpy and hard mats where I kneel, receive, and ponder.

Then I must step away to let another come for that moment unlike any other. I push myself up from the rail, fold my hands together, and walk back, changed, toward the world where I live.[55]

What life have you

if you have not life together?

There is no life that is not in community,

And no community not lived

in praise of GOD.

—T.S. Eliot (1888–1965), bank clerk, poet, and winner of the Nobel Prize for Literature

The Blessed Company

Donald Coggan (1909–2000), *Archbishop of Canterbury from 1974 to 1980, was an evangelical who hoped for intercommunion with Roman Catholics as well as the ordination of women. When the Church of England finally admitted women to the priesthood in 1994, Rome responded by declaring female ordination impossible. Official intercommunion still has not happened.*

"Faith," so the small boy is reported to have said, "is believing what you know to be untrue." His definition is all too close to what many do in fact think about a word that is at the very heart of New Testament Christianity. Shut your eyes, swallow with determination, take a deep breath, and say the Apostles' Creed—*that* is faith! But this is a travesty of the real thing. . . .

When Jesus, walking by the Lake of Galilee, called two brothers and received from them their response ("they rose and followed Him"), that was the beginning of a faith-relationship. Though it may well be that these young men had known Jesus from boyhood, in fact they knew very little about the real significance of the One who so imperiously and yet so graciously called them. But, that great day, they responded with all that they knew of themselves to all that they then knew of Christ. That is faith. It was tiny as a grain of mustard seed. Thirty years later Peter knew a great deal more about Christ (not to say about himself!) than he did on the day of his call. But that is the way of faith. It begins in a small way. It has such vast potentialities of growth.

Faith begins as an intensely personal response to the outgoing love of God manifested supremely in the Christ of Nazareth, of the Cross and of the empty tomb. But it is soon seen to have an equally important corporate aspect. The "believer", the man of faith, finds himself incorporated into "the blessed company of all faithful people", and it is here, within that company, that he finds his nourishment and the secret of his growth. Here the life of faith is strengthened by the ministry of Word and Sacrament. It is "with all God's people" that he comes to grasp "what is the breadth and length and height and depth of the love of Christ and to know it, though it is beyond knowledge" (Ephesians 3:18–19).[55]

Coming to the Sacrament

John Donne (1572–1631), *best known of the metaphysical poets, was raised Catholic in a time when Catholics were likely to be persecuted. Indeed his own brother died in prison for having sheltered a Catholic priest. Not long after, Donne distanced himself from the Catholic Church and found a good job as secretary to a high government official. The official fired him, however, when Donne's secret marriage to the daughter of a wealthy landowner became known, and Donne struggled for many years to support his growing family. Eventually he took Holy Orders in the Church of England—the only regular employment open to him—and became famous for his sermons. For obvious reasons, Donne did not care for theological arguments.*

When thou comest to this seal of thy peace, the Sacrament, pray that God will give thee that light, that may direct and establish thee, in necessary and fundamental things; that is, the light of faith to see, that the body and blood of Christ, is applied to thee, in that action; But for the manner, how the body and blood of Christ is there, wait his leisure, if he have not yet manifested that to thee: Grieve not at that, wonder not at that, press not for that; for he hath not manifested that, not the way, not the manner of his presence in the Sacrament, to the Church. A peremptory prejudice upon other men's opinions, that no opinion but thine can be true, in the doctrine of the Sacrament, and an uncharitable condemning of other men, or other Churches that may be of another persuasion than thou art, in the matter of the Sacrament, may frustrate and disappoint thee of all that benefit, which thou mightest have, by an humble receiving thereof, if thou wouldest exercise thy faith only, here, and leave thy passion at home, and refer thy reason, and disputation to the School.[57]

"This Is My Body"

Elizabeth I (1533–1603), *the younger daughter of Henry VIII, is often credited with this little poem. Others have attributed it to the great poet John Donne, who, like the queen, had no patience with raging theological arguments. The poem echoes the words of St. Thomas Aquinas in his hymn "Pange Lingua": "Word made flesh, the bread he taketh, by his word his Flesh to be; wine his sacred blood he maketh, though the senses fail to see; faith alone the true heart waketh to behold the mystery." Though people have argued for nearly two thousand years about what exactly Christ meant when he said "This is my body," the important thing is not to understand what happens at communion, but to receive Christ's body in faith.*

> He was the Word, that spake it:
> He took the bread and brake it;
> And what that Word did make it,
> I do believe, and take it.[58]

Faith Thrives in Community

Austin Farrer (1904–68) *was an Anglican clergyman, philosopher, and theologian, and a friend of C. S. Lewis. Wanting to show that Christian faith is reasonable even in a scientific age, he wrote many books for laypeople on Christianity. Here he is commenting on Romans 1:11–12: "For I am longing to see you so that I may share with you some spiritual gift to strengthen you—or rather so that we may be mutually encouraged by each other's faith, both yours and mine."*

Believing in God is in fact a common undertaking. It is the greatest of human enterprises, and, like other important enterprises, it is only possible of achievement by common endeavor. Faith is not the possession of the single mind alone, it is the possession of the Church. It is personally real, of course, but it lives by communication and interchange. Sometimes someone says to me, "I try to remember the presence of God when I pray by myself, but it is much easier when I worship together with others." That is not a discovery which would have greatly surprised St. Paul. . . .

But are we not being fooled? Are we not simply

yielding to the suggestions of mass emotions? We might be, of course, but in fact we are not. We have seriously and with consideration accepted Christ. If so, it is absurd for us to say that we will cultivate our faith under no conditions but the most adverse, the most killing and solitary. . . .

Our communion is with Christ, and it is because Christ, by faith, lives in our fellow Christians that our faith lives by communion with theirs, and theirs with ours.[59]

Finding a Faith Community

Debra Farrington, *publisher of Morehouse Publishing, is well known as a writer and leader of spiritual retreats. Confirmed in the Episcopal Church as an adult, she tells the story of her spiritual journey in* Romancing the Holy.

In the rush of our daily lives we often fail to establish or join spiritual communities that focus us more clearly on God and move us away from self-centeredness. If you are an introvert, finding the nurturing communities and making the effort to be active within them can feel like one more thing on the "to-do" list, rather than a source of communion and deep joy. If, however, we attend to our spiritual life outside of community we miss a great deal. Left to our own devices we will develop a comfortable spirituality that fails to challenge us. Perhaps it will be perfectly crafted for our own needs, but leaves out those of others. More than likely it will be a weak theology that does not sustain us in times of deep trouble. Without the community we have little support when things go wrong in our world; without having developed the habit of nurturing as well as challenging others we will be without others to help us celebrate or mourn the important moments in our lives.

. . . Churches, prayer groups, and other spiritual communities are full of people you will adore and people you'll find harder to love. But every one of them is beloved of God and reveals something of God for you to learn and know. Individually and collectively they invite you out of your own world and into the communion of the whole people of God.[60]

Openly Before the Church

The first Book of Common Prayer *was published in 1549, nearly two decades after Henry VIII broke with the Church of Rome. The Archbishop of Canterbury, Thomas Cranmer, was its editor. This statement on confirmation isn't too hard to read if you remember that "i" and "y" are interchangeable, that where we would write "v," the prayer book uses "u," and that spelling is entirely random.*

To thende that confirmacion may be ministred to the more edifying of suche as shall receiue it (according to Sainte Paules doctrine, who teacheth that all thynges should be doen in the churche to the edificacion of the same) it is thought good that none hereafter shall be confirmed, but suche as can say in theyr mother tong, tharticles of the faith the lordes prayer, and the tenne commaundementes; And can also aunswere to suche questions of this short Catechisme, as the Busshop (or suche as he shall appoynte) shall by his discrecion appose them in. And this ordre is most conuenient to be obserued for diuers consideracions.

First because that whan children come to the yeres of discrecion and haue learned what theyr Godfathers and Godmothers promised for them in Baptisme, they may then theselfes with their owne mouth, and with theyr owne consent, openly before the churche ratifie and confesse the same, and also promise that by the grace of God, they will euermore endeuour them-selues faithfully to obserue and kepe such thinges, as they by theyre owne mouth and confession haue assented unto.

Secondly, forasmuch as confirmacion is ministred to them that be Baptised, that by imposicion of han-des, and praier they maye receiue strength and defence against all temptacions to sin, and the assautes of the worlde, and the deuill: it is most mete to be ministred, when children come to that age, that partly by the frayltie of theyr owne fleshe, partly by the assautes of the world and the deuil, they begin to be in daungier to fall into synne.

Thirdly, for that it is agreeable with the usage of the churche in tymes past, wherby it was ordeined, that Confirmacion should bee ministred to them that were of perfecte age, that they beyng instructed in Christes religion, should openly professe theyr owne fayth, and promise to be obedient unto the will of God.

And that no manne shall thynke that anye detri-mente shall come to children by diferryng of theyr confirmacion: he shall knowe for trueth, that it is certayn by Goddes woorde, that children beeyng Baptized (if they departe out of thys lyfe in theyr infancie) are undoubtedly saued.[61]

To be of no church is dangerous.

Religion, of which the rewards are distant,

and which is animated only by faith and

hope, will glide by degrees out of the mind

unless it be invigorated and reimpressed

by external ordinances,

by stated calls to worship,

and the salutary influence of example.

—Samuel Johnson (1709–84),
essayist and lexicographer

The Faith of the Church

Elizabeth Goudge (1900–1984), *whose father was an Anglican priest and a professor at Oxford, was a prolific and popular novelist in the 1940s and '50s. Her 1947 book,* The Little White Horse, *was Harry Potter creator J. K. Rowling's favorite childhood book.*

"Whom do men say that I, the Son of man, am?" Our Lord asked his disciples as they sat together under the trees. . . .

It was Peter who answered, Peter who with all his sin and weakness and failure had such wonderful flashes of heavenly insight. He knew now without a shadow of doubt who it was who was with them, and he answered his Master with the glorious confession of faith which is the foundation stone of the Christian Church. . . .

"Thou art the Christ, the Son of the living God."

This must have been for Our Lord one of the greatest and happiest moments of his earthly life. Here, at last, was the flame of true faith. For so long he had been nursing the flickering sparks of belief in these children of his, only to see them go out again, but now at last the flame was truly alight. It might waver and almost fail in the darkness that was coming upon them all, but it would not quite go out; it would flare up again and light would be lit from light until the faith of the Church was a blaze that went all round the world.[62]

If we had anything like a worthy notion
of our near relation to God,
adopted as we are by baptism
to be his own children in Christ Jesus,
we should then understand
how very near the same adoption
brings us to one another.

—John Keble (1792–1866), priest and poet

Faithful to the Church or to Christ?

Frank T. Griswold, *formerly the Episcopal Bishop of Chicago, has been Presiding Bishop and Primate of The Episcopal Church, USA, since 1998. Educated at Harvard and Oxford, he served three parishes in Pennsylvania before moving to Chicago. He is especially interested in spirituality, literature, evangelism, and ecumenism.*

I remember once talking to a deeply committed lay person who was having a painful reaction to a change in the life of his parish. With trembling voice he exclaimed, "I love the Episcopal Church!" My immediate reaction was one of discomfort. How dangerous, I thought. Did he love the institution? Or, through it, did he love the Risen Christ, the Lord of the Church, who constantly surprises us and unsettles us as we are drawn more and more into Christ's own work of reconciling all things in himself to God? . . .

Saints and heroes of the faith, understanding human frailty, have always had the sober view of the capacities of the institution. Roman Catholic writer Flannery O'Connor once observed that we are crucified by the church. . . . The church does not so much serve to take care of us as it does to unite us to Christ and to oblige us to allow the pattern of Christ's own faithfulness—which took him to the cross and through it into the new reality of resurrection—to become our own. . . .

Insofar as the church-as-institution reveals and mediates the presence of Christ in its members, in its proclamation and preaching, in its sacramental actions and in its self-giving for the sake of the world, it is worthy of our deepest respect and affection.

At the same time, we must remember that the church is always being reformed and conformed to the image of the Risen One. We as living stones are being built up into a spiritual house not of our own design but according to God's boundless imagination.

So, let us rejoice that we are more than an institution. Let us live the life that is ours in Christ with courage, hope and joy. Let us live in expectation that God will accomplish great things through us, not least of which is the healing of our world.[63]

If you will build a glorious church
unto God, see first yourselves
to be in charity with your neighbors,
and suffer not them to be offended
by your works.

—Hugh Latimer (c. 1485–1555), bishop and martyr

Community Began with Commitment

John Macquarrie, *who became an Anglican as an adult, was Lady Margaret Professor of Divinity at Oxford until his retirement in 1986. He is the author of several major theological works.*

It is unfortunate that faith has frequently been equated with belief, and the Church has encouraged this misconception by laying an undue emphasis on correctness of belief and making this the primary criterion of its membership. Obviously, belief is not unimportant, and if a person's beliefs are erroneous, his conduct may be profoundly distorted. But faith is something more inclusive than belief. It is a total attitude toward life, and although belief is a part of this attitude, its essence is to be seen rather in commitment to a way of life. It may be the case that when the commitment is made, all the beliefs implied in it are not yet clear, and it is only in following out the commitment that the beliefs come to be fully and explicitly understood. This is true not only of the individual coming into the community, but of the community itself. The Christian community began with a commitment to Jesus Christ, but it took some centuries to work out the basic beliefs that were already implicit in the act of commitment, and the unfolding of these beliefs still continues.[64]

If any question arise about the faith
of the Scripture,
let them judge by the manifest
and open Scriptures,
not excluding the lay-men:
for there are many found
among the lay-men which are as wise
as the spiritual officers.

—William Tyndale (c. 1494–1536), priest, translator of first English-language Bible

What the Church Could See

Agnes Sanford (1897–1982), *the daughter of a Presbyterian missionary and the wife of an Episcopal rector, suffered from depression for many years until a minister laid hands on her head and prayed for her. She went on to develop a worldwide healing ministry that emphasized personal experience and visualization. She often said that Jesus' hands were tied behind his back because nobody in the churches expected him to do anything.*

Jesus commanded us to pray that the kingdom of heaven come upon earth, and that His will be done on earth even as it is done in heaven. . . .

For this tremendous, incomprehensible event we are told to pray—the time when the knowledge of God will cover the earth as the waters cover the sea—the time when one man will not say to another, "Know ye the Lord?" for all will know the Lord, from the least unto the greatest.

For the coming of this time, we are commanded to pray, and prayer without believing is of no avail. Prayer without faith accomplishes nothing. Therefore, as I pray this prayer, part of the command of the Lord is that with the eyes of faith I see this earth becoming the kingdom of our God and of His Son, that by a tremendous leap of the imagination I look forward to the time when Jesus Himself, in ways that I do not know, shall reign upon this earth.

So He has commanded me, and while I remain here and obey Him, He comforts my soul, not with visions of heaven—heaven can wait—but with visions of God's glory upon this earth.

And yesterday morning for the first time, as I looked out to the misty hills . . . , I could see the light around the trees. I do not know what this light is. But I cannot imagine it or dream it into reality. When it comes, it comes of itself, as though emanating from the very trees and not from me. Though I do not understand it, my heart is greatly rejoiced when I see it, for it testifies to my spirit of the Spirit of God permeating all His universe.

So may the light shine until the very creature—the earth itself—its ugliness turned into beauty, becomes indeed the kingdom of our God and of His Christ.[65]

The Widest Fellowship We Can Find

William Temple (1881–1944) *was a philosopher, theologian, and social reformer, and the author of many books. When he was a teenager, his father became Archbishop of Canterbury. Forty-seven years later, during World War II, William himself was made the 98th Archbishop of Canterbury.*

No man can be a good Christian by himself. No man is able to understand more than a tiny fraction of the unsearchable riches of Christ; he needs the supplementing contribution of his neighbour's apprehension. And as it is true that no individual alone can be a really good Christian, so it is true that the full Christian life cannot be lived only in groups of like-minded Christians; for if they are like-minded they merely strengthen one another in those elements of Christian faith and experience in which they are already fairly strong. That is good as far as it goes, and these associations have their perfectly real place, for they generate a degree of enthusiasm and zeal which it is perhaps impossible to produce in the wider fellowship of the Church if it has no such lesser fellowships within it. But if such associations keep themselves apart from, and do not freely mingle with, other associations of people whose apprehension of Christ has been other than their own, they tend to stereotype their limitations as well as strengthen their faith, and in the end they may easily become causes of division, which weaken the whole Church in its witness, and so may even do harm as great as the good they do. It must be in the widest fellowship we can find, and a fellowship that bears the promise of permanence from age to age, that we are to fulfil the obligations of our membership.[66]

Notes

1. Dennis Bennett, *Moving Right Along in the Spirit* (Old Tappan, N.J.: Revell, 1983), 97–99.

2. Richard Nelson Bolles, *What Color Is Your Parachute?: A Practical Manual for Job-Hunters and Career-Changers* (Berkeley, Calif.: Ten Speed, 2003), 315–16.

3. Robert Farrar Capon, *The Third Peacock: A Book about God and the Problem of Evil* (Garden City, N.Y.: Doubleday, 1971), 116–17.

4. George Carey, *A Tale of Two Churches: Can Protestants and Catholics Get Together?* (Downers Grove, Ill.: InterVarsity, 1985), 72–73.

5. Lewis Carroll, *Through the Looking Glass and What Alice Found There* (New York: Heritage, 1941), 91.

6. Barbara Cawthorne Crafton, *Let Every Heart Prepare: Meditations for Advent and Christmas* (Harrisburg, Pa.: Morehouse Publishing, 1998), 59–60.

7. Thomas Cranmer, *Book of Homilies*, 1547.

8. Alan Jones, *Passion for Pilgrimage: Notes for the Journey Home* (Harrisburg, Pa.: Morehouse Publishing, 1989), 39.

9. William Law, *Of Justification by Faith and Works: A Dialogue Between a Methodist and a Churchman*, paragraphs 4 and 5.

10. Kenneth Leech, *True Prayer: An Invitation to Christian Spirituality* (Harrisburg, Pa: Morehouse Publishing, 1980, 1995), 44–46.

11. Mark McIntosh, *Mysteries of Faith*, vol. 8, The New Church's Teaching Series (Boston: Cowley, 2000), 100–101.

12. John Newton, *Cardiphonia; or, The Utterance of the Heart, in the Course of a Real Correspondence* (1781); from eight letters to the Rev. Mr. S——, Letter VII, 17 November 1775.

13. J. I. Packer, *Growing in Christ* (1977; Wheaton, Ill.: Crossway, 1994), 19–20.

14. Dorothy L. Sayers, *The Whimsical Christian* (New York: Collier, 1987), 29–30.

15. John Stott, *Understanding the Bible*, quoted in Timothy Dudley-Smith, ed., *Authentic Christianity: From the Writings of John Stott* (Downers Grove, Ill.: InterVarsity, 1995), 176.

16. Jeremy Taylor, *The Rule and Exercises of Holy Living* (Philadelphia: Bradley, 1860), ch. 4, sec. 1.

17. Steve Turner, *Imagine: A Vision for Christians in the Arts* (Downers Grove, Ill.: InterVarsity, 2001), 108–9.

18. Desmond Tutu, "The Divine Intention," *Hope and Suffering: Sermons and Speeches* (Grand Rapids, Mich. Eerdmans, 1983), 176–77.

19. Evelyn Underhill, *The Spiritual Life* (1937; reprint, Harrisburg, Pa.: Morehouse Publishing, 1995), 51–52.

20. Robert E. Webber, *Evangelicals on the Canterbury Trail: Why Evangelicals Are Attracted to the Liturgical Church* (Waco, Tex.: Word/Jarrell, 1985), 14–15.

21. Charles Williams, *Descent of the Dove: A Short History of the Holy Spirit in the Church* (1939; reprint, Grand Rapids, Mich.: Eerdmans, 1980), 8–10.

22. David Adam, *The Open Gate: Celtic Prayers for Growing Spiritually* (Harrisburg, Pa.: Morehouse Publishing, 1994), 1, 2, 3.

23. Mortimer J. Adler, *How to Think about God: A Guide for the 20th-Century Pagan* (New York: Macmillan, 1980), 155, 158.

24. Agatha Christie, *An Autobiography* (1977; reprint, New York: Berkley Books, 1996), 14–15.

25. L. William Countryman, *Forgiven and Forgiving* (Harrisburg, Pa.: Morehouse Publishing, 1998), 19.

26. Esther de Waal, *Living with Contradiction: An Introduction to Benedictine Spirituality* (Harrisburg, Pa.: Morehouse Publishing, 1989, 1997), 138–39.

27. Elisabeth Elliot, *The Savage My Kinsman* (Ann Arbor, Mich.: Servant, 1961, 1981, and 1996), 63.

28. Timothy Jones, *Awake My Soul: Practical Spirituality for Busy People* (New York: Doubleday, 1999), 2–3.

29. J. B. Phillips, *Your God Is Too Small* (New York: Macmillan, 1965), 126–28.

30. John Polkinghorne, *The Faith of a Physicist: Reflections of a Bottom-Up Thinker* (1994; reprint, Minneapolis: Fortress, 1996), 37–38.

31. John Updike, "Pigeon Feathers," *Pigeon Feathers and Other Stories* (New York: Fawcett Crest, 1959, 1960, 1961, 1962), 105.

32. Frank R. VanDevelder, *The Biblical Journey of Faith: The Road of the Sojourner* (Philadelphia: Fortress, 1988), 111.

33. John Wesley, *The Journal of John Wesley*, Wednesday, 24 May 1738.

34. Rowan Williams The Archbishop of Canterbury, *Christmas Day Meditation 2002*; http://www.archbishopofcanterbury.org /sermons_speeches/021225.html.

35. Randall Balmer, *Growing Pains: Learning to Love My Father's Faith* (Grand Rapids, Mich.: Brazos, 2001), 33–34.

36. Nevada Barr, *Seeking Enlightenment Hat by Hat* (New York: Putnam, 2003), 154–55.

37. Diana Butler Bass, *Strength for the Journey: A Pilgrimage of Faith in Community* (San Francisco: Jossey-Bass, 2002), 281–82.

38. William Cowper, "Light Shining Out of Darkness," *Olney Hymns* (1779).

39. Elizabeth II, "The Queen's Christmas Message: 25 December 2002"; http://www.britain=info.org/ monarchy/xq/asp/SarticleType.1/Article_ID.3007/qx/articles_show.htm.

40. Nora Gallagher, *Things Seen and Unseen: A Year Lived in Faith* (New York: Vintage, 1998), 78–79.

41. Gail Godwin, *Evensong* (New York: Ballantine, 1999), 12.

42. George Herbert, "Faith," *George Herbert: The Country Parson, The Temple*, John N. Wall, Jr., ed., *The Classics of Western Spirituality* (Mahwah, N.Y.: Paulist, 1981), 164.

43. Richard Hooker, *Of the Laws of Ecclesiastical Polity*, 2 vols. (New York: Dutton, 1907), I:6–7.

44. Susan Howatch, on-line interview with *Bookends*, n.d.; http://www.bookends.co.uk/bookends/chat/howatch.asp.

45. Madeleine L'Engle, *The Irrational Season* (San Francisco: HarperSanFrancisco, 1977), 29, 34.

46. C. S. Lewis, *The Lion, the Witch and the Wardrobe* (New York: HarperCollins, 1950), chap. 8, "What Happened After Dinner."

47. Margaret Duggan, ed., *Through the Year with Michael Ramsey: Devotional Readings for Every Day* (Grand Rapids, Mich.: Eerdmans, 1977; London: Hodder and Stoughton, 1975), 15.

48. Robert A. K. Runcie, "Easter, 1981," *Seasons of the Spirit: The Archbishop of Canterbury at Home and Abroad* (Grand Rapids, Mich.: Eerdmans, 1983), 68.

49. Luci Shaw, *Postcard from the Shore* (Wheaton, Ill.: Harold Shaw, 1985), 46.

50. Alexandra Stoddard, *Feeling at Home: Defining Who You Are and How You Want to Live* (New York: William Morrow, 1999), xv.

51. Alfred Lord Tennyson, *In Memoriam*, OBIIT MDCC-CXXXIII and LV.

52. Phyllis Tickle, *A Stitch and a Prayer: A Memoir of Faith Amidst War* (Brewster, Mass.: Paraclete, 2003), 26–28.

53. Robert Benson, *Between the Dreaming and the Coming True: The Road Home to God* (San Francisco: HarperSanFrancisco, 1996), 24–25.

54. Phillips Brooks, *Selected Sermons*, ed. William Scarlett (New York: Dutton, 1950), 48–49.

55. Kate Young Caley, *The House Where the Hardest Things Happened: A Memoir about Belonging* (New York: Doubleday, 2002), 157–58.

56. Donald Coggan, *Convictions* (Grand Rapids, Mich.: Eerdmans, 1975), 170–71.

57. John Donne, "From a sermon preached on Christmas Day 1626 [Transubstatiation]," *John Donne: The Major Works*, ed. John Carey (New York: Oxford University Press, 1990), 374–75.

58. The translation of "Pange lingua" is from *The Hymnal 1982* (New York: Church Publishing Incorporated, 1985), 329.

59. Austin Farrer, *A Faith of Our Own* (Cleveland: World, 1960), 48–49, 51.

60. Debra Farrington, *Living Faith Day by Day: How the Sacred Rules of Monastic Traditions Can Help You Live Spiritually in the Modern World* (New York: Perigee, 2000), 157–58.

61. The Booke of the Common Prayer and Administracion of the Sacramentes, and Other Rites and Ceremonies of the Churche after the Use of the Churche of England (1549), quoted in *The First and Second Prayer Books of Edward VI* (London: J. M. Dent & Sons, 1910), 247.

62. Elizabeth Goudge, *God So Loved the World: The Story of Jesus* (New York: Coward-McCann, 1951), 188.

63. Frank T. Griswold, "And What Is 'Church'?" *Episcopal Life* (July/August 2002); http://www.episcopalchurch.org/episcopal-life/PB7'02.html.

64. John Macquarrie, *The Faith of the People of God: A Lay Theology* (New York: Scribner's, 1972), 27–28.

65. Agnes Sanford, *Sealed Orders* (Plainfield, N.J.: Logos International, 1972), 312–13.

66. William Temple, *Christian Faith and Life* (New York: Macmillan, 1931), 127–28.

List of Contributors

Permissions

Excerpt from *Moving Right Along in the Spirit* by Dennis Bennett. Copyright © 1983 by Dennis Bennett. Reprinted by permission of Rita Bennett. Rita Bennett, Dennis's widow, continues as President and C.E.O. of Christian Renewal Association, Inc., in Edmonds, Washington 98020; website: www.EmotionallyFree.org. Her upcoming book of prose, memoirs, and poetry *Treasures from an Oak Chest* will be published through CRA in August 2003.

Reprinted with permission from WHAT COLOR IS YOUR PARACHUTE? by Richard Nelson Bolles. Copyright © 2003 by Richard Nelson Bolles, Ten Speed Press, Berkeley, CA. Available from your local bookseller, by calling Ten Speed Press at 800-841-2665, or by visiting us online at www.tenspeed.com. Visit Richard Nelson Bolles at www.jobhuntersbible.com.

Robert Farrar Capon, from "The Third Peacock," in *The Romance of the Word*, © 1995 Wm. B. Eerdmans Publishing Co., Grand Rapids, MI. Reprinted by permission.

Copyright 2000, Mark McIntosh. All rights reserved. Excerpt is reprinted from *Mysteries of Faith* by Mark McIntosh; Published by Cowley Publications, 907 Massachusetts Avenue, Cambridge, MA 02139. www.cowley.org (800-225-1524).

THE LION, THE WITCH AND THE WARDROBE by C. S. Lewis, copyright © C. S. Lewis Pte. Ltd. 1950. Extract reprinted by permission.

"Faith" from *Postcard from the Shore* by Luci Shaw, Copyright © 1985. Reprinted by permission of Luci Shaw.

Excerpt from p. xv from FEELING AT HOME by ALEXANDRA STODDARD. COPYRIGHT © 1999 BY ALEXANDRA STODDARD. Reprinted by permission of HarperCollins Publishers, Inc. William Morrow. For Additional Territory: Brandt & Brandt, 1501 Broadway, New York, NY 10036.

Excerpt from *A Stitch and a Prayer: A Memoir of Faith Amidst War* by *Phyllis Tickle*. Copyright © 2003 by Phyllis Tickle. Reprinted by permission of Paraclete Press, Inc., Orleans, MA.

Excerpt from *The House Where the Hardest Things Happened: A Memoir about Belonging* by Kate Young Caley © 2002 by Kate Young Caley. Published by Doubleday. Reprinted by permission.

Excerpt from *Convictions* by Donald Coggan, © 1971. Reprinted by permission of Hodder & Stoughton Limited.

Excerpt from *Living Faith Day by Day: How the Sacred Rules of Monastic Traditions Can Help You Live Spiritually in the Modern World* by Debra Farrington, © 2000 by Debra Farrington. Published by Perigee. Reprinted by permission.

Excerpt from GOD SO LOVED THE WORLD: THE STORY OF JESUS by Elizabeth Goudge © 1951. Published by Hodder & Stoughton. Reprinted by permission of David Higham Associates Limited.

FAITH OF THE PEOPLE OF GOD by Macquarrie, © 1972. Reprinted by permission of Pearson Education, Inc., Upper Saddle River, NJ.

Excerpt from *Sealed Orders* by Agnes Sanford. Copyright © 1972 by Agnes Sanford. Reprinted by permission of Bridge-Logos Publishers.